STACK
PRESENTS

BASEBALL
TRAINING

D1312363

FOR THE ATHLETE,
BY THE ATHLETE

TRIUMPH
BOOKS

This book is available in quantity at special discounts for your group or organization.
For further information, contact:
Triumph Books
542 South Dearborn Street
Suite 750
Chicago, Illinois 60605
(312) 939–3330
Fax (312) 663–3557
www.triumphbooks.com

Printed in U.S.A.
ISBN: 978-1-60078-366-1

Design, page production, and editing: Red Line Editorial

Project Manager: Rachel Trem

Contributing Writers:
Chad Zimmerman
Josh Staph
Chip Smith
Scott Mackar
Zac Clark
Matt Siracusa
Kyle Woody

Photos courtesy STACK Media unless otherwise indicated.

ABOUT STACK

STACK is the nation's leading producer and distributor of sports performance, training, and lifestyle content for high school and college athletes and the high school sports community. Founded by Nick Palazzo and Chad Zimmerman, two former collegiate football athletes, STACK has the singular goal of improving the lives of athletes by providing safe and effective advice on how to properly boost performance without the use of steroids or other illegal performance enhancing drugs.

The name STACK stands for the complete "stack" of information an athlete needs to be more successful in all aspects of life. Key components are STACK's information, instruction, and advice on training and nutrition, which help athletes improve their physical being and performance. But STACK also addresses important life skills and teaches lessons in areas such as team-building, goal-setting, mental preparation, and overcoming adversity. Finally, a very important part of STACK's content mix is material related to college selection and the recruiting process, including tips and advice on character building, presenting oneself properly to coaches, and focusing on strong academics.

STACK's content does not come from individuals who claim to be "experts," but have little experience working with elite athletes. On the contrary, the information and advice provided by STACK comes directly from today's best athletes and the experts who work with them on a regular basis. Athletes such as Peyton Manning, LeBron James, Johan Santana, LaDainian Tomlinson, Allen Iverson, and Tim Duncan have willingly made their training, nutrition, or personal experiences available to STACK's audience. Why? Because they want to support STACK's mission of helping athletes safely improve their performance. By using star professional athletes as role models, STACK produces content that's real, raw, and authentic and makes a powerful, lasting impression on its readers and viewers.

CONTENTS

INTRODUCTION

How is this Book Different?

This book is a compilation of the best baseball workouts published in *STACK* Magazine since the company was launched in 2005. Over the past four and a half years, STACK content directors have observed hundreds of workouts by some of the best professional and collegiate players and strength coaches in the business. In the following pages, you'll gain exclusive insights into how successful pros such as Carl Crawford, Derrek Lee, Justin Morneau, and Dustin Pedroia prepare their bodies to perform at peak levels during the long and demanding MLB season. Unlike those in some other publications, these workouts are real. They are the exact regimens used by each featured MLB star every day, week, month, and year. The impeccable, polished product you see on the field every day is crafted—with little or no fanfare—in the gym, on the practice field, on the track. If you want to know how these men were shaped into formidable athletes, read on.

What is STACK?

STACK is the nation's leading producer and distributor of sports performance, training, and lifestyle content for active sports participants.

Recognizing the need—and in response to the demand—for state-of-the-art sports performance information, Nick Palazzo and Chad Zimmerman, two former collegiate football players, launched STACK in February 2005. Their singular goal was to improve the lives of young athletes by providing safe and effective advice on how to boost performance without the use of steroids or other illegal performance enhancing drugs. Since the company's founding, the STACK editorial team, which produces all of the company's original content, has been forging relationships with the best and brightest in the sports performance, sports nutrition, strength and conditioning, recruiting, sports psychology, and related fields, all of which are vital to developing a well-rounded athlete. Via recorded interviews and video shoots, more than 400 experts have contributed to STACK's content library, providing readers and website visitors with easy access to the cutting-edge and groundbreaking techniques that help already-elite athletes get even better. This access is what separates STACK from other media properties and what makes STACK's content real, raw, and authentic.

STACK's Objectives

The three pillars of STACK's mission to athletes are to provide:
- Information, instruction, and advice on training and nutrition, which help athletes enhance physical well being, improve on-field performance, and avoid injury
- Emphasis on important life skills, which teach lessons in areas such as team-building, goal-setting, mental preparation, and overcoming adversity
- Advice on the college selection and recruiting process, including tips and suggestions on character building, presenting oneself properly to coaches, and focusing on strong academics.

STACK Platforms

STACK reaches its ever-expanding audience through STACK Media, *STACK* Magazine, STACK.com, STACK TV, and MySTACK.

STACK Media is one of the top sports properties on the Internet, with an average of four million unique visitors and 100 million page views per month, according to comScore. Recognizing that active young males are hard to reach online, STACK Media combines its unique and appealing editorial content with product and service offerings from a number of related partner sites to fully engage its audience through a distributed media network. From its origins as a magazine publisher, STACK Media has become the acknowledged leader in reaching active sports participants online.

STACK Magazine, requested by more than 9,000 high school athletic directors, has a circulation of 800,000 and a readership of nearly five million high school athletes. In keeping with the company's mission, the magazine is devoted to helping shape well-rounded athletes now and in the future. Published six times throughout the school year, the magazine is loaded with expert advice from top professional athletes and their trainers. STACK Magazine teaches young athletes the proper way to train, eat, and develop their skills, while also educating them on how to be good teammates, respect their opponents, and handle adversity—lessons based on the experiences of pro and college athletes who have reached the pinnacle of success in their sports.

STACK.com, the digital home for all STACK content and web-based tools, provides content exclusively for youth sports participants. With coverage of more than 20 sports and content featuring lifestyle information as well as training, nutrition, and sports skills, the site offers something for everyone with an interest in sports performance.

STACK TV, an online platform with eight channels and several categories of unique, proprietary videos, constitutes the largest video library of sports performance content on the web. More than 4,000 (and counting) videos feature top professional and collegiate athletes, coaches, trainers, and sports nutritionists, all offering the benefits of their expertise to young athletes seeking to improve their performance.

MySTACK is a social network and recruiting site that allows athletes to create profiles with their personal information and stats, upload highlight films and photos, and send their profiles to college coaches. Tens of thousands of athletes have signed up as MySTACK members, and many use the network to connect (and compete) with each other as well as to take control of the recruiting process, confirming the proposition that competition breeds success.

STACK EXPERTS

CRAIG FRIEDMAN
Athletes' Performance
athletesperformance.com

As a performance specialist for Athletes' Performance, Craig Friedman designs and implements training programs for professional baseball, football, tennis, soccer, and basketball players, as well as for elite younger athletes at all levels. He earned both his bachelor and master of science degrees from the University of Tennessee, Knoxville, while working in the school's Women's Athletic Training Department. After leaving Tennessee, he signed on with the University of Arizona as assistant athletic trainer for football. Friedman has given performance-training lectures at conferences and in classrooms, both nationally and internationally. Athletes' Performance pro baseball clients include Carl Crawford, Curt Schilling, Eric Chavez, and Jason Varitek.

AL BIANCANI
Biancani Fitness Training
Founder and Owner
biancanifitness.com

biancanifitness.com

A veteran of the strength and conditioning field for more than 30 years, Al Biancani operates Biancani Fitness Training in addition to serving as strength coach for the Sacramento Kings and Sacramento Monarchs. Biancani helps high school, college, and professional athletes to achieve their personal best.

JAVAIR GILLETT
Detroit Tigers
Strength and conditioning coach
detroittigers.com

Since taking the reins of the Tigers' strength and conditioning program in 2005, Javair Gillett has overseen the team's entire program, from in-season strength maintenance to individualized off-season conditioning for each player. He is a certified strength and conditioning specialist through the National Strength and Conditioning Association.

Gillett created the B.A.S.E.S training program, which stands for Balance, Agility, Strength, Explosiveness, and Speed. Through www.prosactive.com, videos, and a DVD, *B.A.S.E.S.: Evolution of an Athlete*, the program helps athletes improve performance, prevent injury, and decrease the likelihood of disease.

Gillett started his career with Detroit's Double-A team in Erie, Pennsylvania, and Triple-A team in Toledo, Ohio. He also interned with the Orlando Magic for the 2002–03 season. He holds a bachelor's degree in exercise science from DePauw University. During his collegiate baseball career, Gillett was a two-time All-Southern Collegiate Athletic Conference first baseman.

MARK VERSTEGEN
Athletes' Performance
Founder, chairman
athletesperformance.com

Mark Verstegen is one of the world's most innovative sports performance experts. As the owner of Athletes' Performance training centers in Tempe, Arizona, Carson, California, and Gulf Breeze, Florida, he directs a team of performance specialists and nutritionists who work with world-class athletes from all sports. Verstegen, who also serves as director of performance for the NFL Players Association and as a consultant to other athletic governing bodies, earned his bachelor's in exercise science from Washington State University and his master's in sports science from the University of Idaho. In 1994, he created the International Performance Institute on the campus of the IMG Sports Academy in Bradenton, Florida.

CHIP SMITH
Competitive Edge Sports
Founder
competitiveedgesports.com

Considered one of the forefathers of the sports training industry, Chip Smith has trained more than 300 NFL players during his career. His impressive football clientele, most of whom train at Smith's Competitive Edge Sports facility [Duluth, Georgia], includes 39 Pro Bowl players, 20 first-round draft picks, three Heisman Trophy winners, and 25 NCAA All-Americans. A two-sport athlete [football and baseball] at Liberty University, Smith still holds rushing and scoring records. In the mid-1980s, he studied at the famed Soviet Sports Institute upon invitation, and he has headed the U.S. Olympic Power Lifting team.

AARON SISTRUNK
Perfect Fitt
Owner
perfectfitt.com

Aaron Sistrunk's primary duty is
serving as strength and conditioning
coach for Chestnut Hill Academy
in Philadelphia. In addition to
Perfect Fitt, he also co-owns Balance Chestnut Hill, LLC.
Sistrunk works with all athletes, from elite professionals to
young children, employing a contrast method of training
to improve body control and core stability. Sistrunk
graduated from Wesley College with a bachelor's degree
in physical education, and he holds certifications in sports
nutrition and professional training from the International
Fitness Professional Association. He is a specialist in sports
conditioning, as certified by the International Sports Science
Association.

MILT THOMPSON
Philadelphia Phillies
Hitting Coach
phillies.com

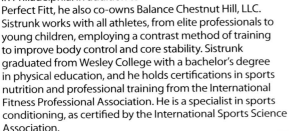

After coaching stints with minor
league affiliates of the Tampa Bay
Rays and the Philadelphia Phillies,
Milt Thompson returned to the majors in 2003 as the Phillies'
first base coach. A year later, as hitting coach, he improved
the team's batting average and on-base percentage while
lowering the number of strikeouts for the season. In his
second year as hitting coach, the Phillies led the National
League in runs [865], runs batted in [823], and walks [626]. A
left fielder, Thompson spent 11 years in the big leagues with
several teams before retiring in 1996. During the 1993 World
Series, he hit .313 with six RBIs as a member of the Phillies.

PERRY CASTELLANO
Minnesota Twins
Major League strength and
conditioning coordinator
twinsbaseball.com

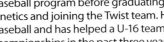

Perry Castellano has served for
eight years in professional baseball,
including three with the Minnesota
Twins. Responsible for the Twins' in-season and off-season
fitness and wellness programs, he embraces a ground-
based philosophy of training to develop flexibility, core
stability, balance, and lower-body strength to support body
weight and maintain each player's strength throughout
the season. Castellano is also a senior sports performance
coach at Velocity Sports Performance, where he specializes
in teaching running mechanics to athletes of all ages and

skill levels. He has worked in sports for more than 20 years,
and is a registered coach with the National Strength and
Conditioning Association.

PETER TWIST
Twist Conditioning, Inc.
President and CEO
twistconditioning.com

Peter Twist is the founder, president,
and CEO of Twist Conditioning, Inc.,
one of Canada's premier fitness
companies, providing athletic
performance enhancement products, education, and
services. A former NHL strength coach for 11 years, Twist has
worked with more than 700 professional athletes during his
career. In addition to his hands-on work with athletes, he is an
avid educator, having authored seven books, 16 DVDs, and
more than 400 articles on sport conditioning.

MIKI KAWAHARA
Twist Conditioning, Inc.
Manager of baseball conditioning
twistconditioning.com

Miki Kawahara is a senior strength
and conditioning coach and the
manager of baseball conditioning
at Twist Conditioning, Inc. Kawahara
was a part of the University of British Columbia [NAIA]
baseball program before graduating with a degree in human
kinetics and joining the Twist team. He continues to coach
baseball and has helped a U-16 team, winning two regional
championships in the past three years.

DEAN SHIELS
Twist Conditioning, Inc.
Vice president of athlete training
services
twistconditioning.com

Dean Shiels is the vice president
of athlete training services at Twist
Conditioning, Inc. He oversees more
than 1,000 amateur and professional athletes who participate
in Twist's training programs each year. An Academic All-
Canadian at the University of British Columbia, Shiels now
travels across North America educating and presenting to
fitness professionals.

CHAPTER 1

CARL CRAWFORD

EDITOR'S NOTE

Carl Crawford's consistent league-leading stolen base output makes him one of the most impressive athletes in professional baseball. But although he was a favorite among fantasy players, Crawford did not achieve wide acclaim from a large fan base—until the 2009 All-Star game.

In the bottom of the seventh, with the score tied 3–3, the Tampa Bay leftfielder made a jaw-dropping, leaping catch over the top of the wall, robbing Colorado's Brad Hawpe of a game-changing home run. The feat earned Crawford the game's MVP Award and confirmed his status as one of MLB's most gifted athletes.

We knew this four years earlier after witnessing the off-season training that Crawford performed to maintain and improve his athletic gifts. Working with the masterminds at Athletes' Performance in Tempe, Arizona, Crawford challenged his mind as well as his body to get the most out of his game. Focusing on strength and mobility, Crawford has made himself stronger, faster, and healthier so he can continue to tear up the basepaths and menace hitters from the outfield.

This is the Carl Crawford cover feature as it originally appeared in the March 2005 issue of *STACK* Magazine.

CARL CRAWFORD FOLLOWS THROUGH ON A HOME-RUN SWING DURING A GAME IN 2009. CRAWFORD DRIVES OPPONENTS CRAZY WITH BOTH HIS POWER AND HIS SPEED.

CARL CRAWFORD CRACKS THE CODE

Although Carl Crawford faced some of the typical and exciting decisions most high school seniors make—like what classes to schedule and who to take to prom—his life-after-high school choice was quite different. In fact, it was one of the biggest decisions of his life thus far.

In 1999, his graduating year, Crawford posted one of the most successful seasons for an option quarterback in high school football history. For that, he earned a full ride to Nebraska. That same year, after an amazing basketball season in which he averaged more than 25 points a game, Crawford had the opportunity to pursue the sport for UCLA— one of the most storied college basketball programs in the country. Crawford closed out his high school athletic career with a stellar baseball season, which resulted in the chance to pursue the game professionally. The Tampa Bay Devil Rays snatched him in the second round of the 1999 draft.

He turned down football at Nebraska, declined a basketball career with the Bruins, and chose baseball. And just five years later, he was selected as a member of the 2004 American League All-Star team.

In 2002, Crawford made another decision that he now thinks of as one of his best. He started training with Athletes' Performance [AP]. "I would rate my decision to train at Athletes' Performance as one of the best decisions I have ever made," Crawford says.

AP, an elite training facility in Tempe, Ariz., has trained top professional, collegiate and high school athletes including NFL veteran Kevin Hardy, world-renown soccer player Mia Hamm and former Boston Red Sox pitcher Curt Schilling. Each one of these athletes has testified

to the improved strength and conditioning that AP has facilitated. Crawford is no exception. "I'm more flexible, my running form is better and the workouts make me mentally tough," he says.

Craig Friedman, the performance specialist who heads the facility's baseball program development and implementation, explains the progress Crawford has made as an AP athlete. "Carl has made huge strides in learning more about his body, specifically in regards to improving his stabilizing strength, which has allowed him truly to start to harness his ability. Over the years, he has continued to focus his energies into incredible speed, elasticity and strength that would athletically rate him in the very top of Major League Baseball, especially as it pertains to his style of play."

As a testament to his dedication to improvement, Crawford bought a home in Arizona. He now trains at AP for the majority of the off-season with two workouts a day, five days a week. AP tailors the workouts for Crawford's body as a baseball player.

"It is essential to train baseball athletes rotationally. Rotational medicine ball throws and rotational lifts such as cable rows, chops and lifts help the athlete engage the back hip as the trigger to developing proper linking for rotational movements. Improving this firing pattern has a huge carryover to hitting and throwing," Friedman explains.

To produce a program that accomplishes these results, AP incorporates eight key elements into a two-part training routine— prehab, movement prep, movement skills, plyos, medicine balls, strength, regeneration, and Energy System Developments [ESD]. The morning session integrates prehab, movement prep, movement skills, and plyos. A regeneration segment completes the session. Medicine ball, strength and ESD are part of the afternoon session, which also wraps up with a regeneration unit. Each of the eight elements has different drills, which should be performed on different days. The workout as a whole also should evolve throughout the off-season. The following drills comprise one day of Crawford's elemental training. Each drill is defined under its respective training element.

HIP PREHAB

1 MINIBAND WALK—LATERAL BENT

- Wrap miniband around both ankles

- Shuffle laterally left 15 steps; repeat to right

COACHING POINTS

- ➡ Keep each step slow and controlled
- ➡ Keep bend in knees at all times
- ➡ Keep back flat and abs tight

2 PRONE HIP INTERNAL ROTATION

- Lying on ground on stomach, bend legs at knees so bottoms of feet face ceiling

- Partner grabs feet and gently pushes legs apart so that each leg rotates externally to slight point of tension

- Resist partner by pushing feet together

COACHING POINTS

- ➡ Keep legs in 90-degree bend throughout drill
- ➡ Give enough resistance to force partner to rotate legs slowly

3 DIAGONAL ARM LIFT — KNEES

- Get on all fours on ground

- Lift hand off ground and extend arm diagonally from body

- Switch arms; repeat for specified reps

COACHING POINTS

- ➡ Keep lower back and abs tight
- ➡ Avoid any pronounced weight shift in body

4 FOUR-WAY HIP CABLE

Set cable at low position and secure cuff around right ankle. Perform following specified reps

- Face away from cable pulley machine, drive right knee up and forward to hip level, bringing knee to 90 degrees

- Face cable pulley machine and drive right leg back, keeping it straight

- Stand with cable pulley machine to left, drive right leg away from pulley, keeping it straight

- Stand with cable pulley machine to right, drive right leg left across body, keeping it straight

- Repeat variations with left leg

COACHING POINT

➡ Properly position body for each movement so pulley resists direction of your kick

5 BALANCE

- Stand on one leg on swivel board or any unstable surface

- Balancing, go through four-way hip movements from previous drill

- Switch legs; repeat movements balancing on opposite leg

COACHING POINTS

➡ Begin drill with no resistance
➡ As balance improves, use four-way hip cable to increase difficulty

PILLAR BRIDGE FRONT

- Lie on ground with forearms on ground under chest

- Flexing abs and lower back, raise hips off ground so only forearms and toes are on floor

- Hold for specified time

COACHING POINT

➤ Keep body in flat plane from head to toes

PILLAR BRIDGE LATERAL

- Lie on ground on side with legs stacked on top of each other

- Place forearm on ground under shoulder, slightly raising upper body off ground

- Lift hips off ground; hold for specified time

- Switch sides

COACHING POINT

➤ Keep abs and lower back contracted at all times
➤ Maintain straight line from feet to shoulders

MOVEMENT PREP—TURF

Spend 20 minutes per day on movement prep.

1 FORWARD LUNGE ELBOW TO INSTEP

- Step forward with one foot into lunge position

- Lower hips until back knee is one to two inches off ground; contract glutes

- Without letting front knee move past toes, bring same elbow as forward leg to instep of foot

- Repeat with opposite leg

COACHING POINTS

➡ Lunge to comfortable distance
➡ Keep head up
➡ Do not let knee touch ground

2 BACKWARD LUNGE AND TWIST

- Step backward with one foot into lunge position

- Lower hips until back knee is one to two inches off ground

- Without letting front knee move past toes, reach arm opposite front leg overhead and twist upper body toward front leg to point of slight tension

COACHING POINTS

➡ Keep head up at all times
➡ Do not let knee touch ground

3 LEG CRADLE

- Step forward with left leg

- Raise right knee as you rotate leg to bring right foot toward left hand

- Grab right foot with left hand and right knee with right hand

- Keeping lower portion of right leg parallel to floor, pull right leg into stomach and flex left glute

- Repeat with left leg

COACHING POINT

➡ The line from foot to knee should be parallel with ground

4 KNEE HUGS

- Step forward with one foot; bring opposite knee to chest

- Grab raised knee with both hands, pulling it as close to chest as possible

- Rise onto toes, tightening glute of that leg

- Repeat on opposite side; continue in alternating fashion for specified distance

COACHING POINTS

➡ Keep chest up and back flat
➡ Pull knee as high as possible
➡ Stay controlled throughout drill

STRENGTH

1 PHYSIOBALL HANGING KNEE-UP

- Lie with lower back on physioball, holding on to stable object behind head

- Keeping legs bent 90 degrees, lower them with control until feet nearly touch floor

- Raise legs and curl body to bring knees above chest

- Repeat for specified reps

COACHING POINTS

➥ Use lower abs to pull knees to chest

➥ Focus on maintaining balance

2 BARBELL RDL

- With feet slightly wider than shoulder width and slight bend in knees, hold barbell with palms facing body at thigh level

- Bend only at hips to lower weight to mid-shin level and continue to push hips back to keep bar close to body

- Return to start position; repeat for specified reps

COACHING POINTS

➥ Do not round lower back

➥ Do not bend knees while lowering weight

➥ Keep head up

3 A-SKIP

- In continuous fashion, skip with proper mechanics, bringing lead knee to waist level and driving foot into ground explosively

- Repeat for specified reps

COACHING POINTS

- Keep head up and facing forward
- Skip as quickly as possible

4 SPLIT-SQUAT—FOOT UP

- Holding dumbbell in each hand, put one foot on bench placed behind you and slightly bend standing knee. You should be one to two feet in front of bench, enough room to squat

- Keeping core tight, squat straight down

- Drive up into starting position by pushing through heel of front foot

- Repeat for specified reps; switch legs

COACHING POINTS

- Keep back flat and chest up at all times
- Do not allow front knee to move past toes
- Keep eyes forward and entire foot in contact with floor

5 REACTIVE STEP-UP

- Place one foot flat on six- to 10-inch box; keep other foot on ground behind box

- Using only leg on box, push down through box to jump upward

- Switch legs in mid-air, so opposite foot lands on box

- Without pausing, immediately perform next step

- Repeat for specified reps

COACHING POINTS

- Jump off box as quickly as possible
- Keep head up
- Use arms for momentum

6 PHYSIOBALL RUSSIAN TWIST

- Lie on physioball so shoulder blades are on ball and hips are off

- With feet flat on ground and knees bent, hold plate over chest with extended arms

- Rotate upper body left, then right, always keeping back in contact with ball

- Repeat for specified reps

COACHING POINTS

- ➡ Tighten core to help balance
- ➡ Keep arms locked out at all times
- ➡ Use light weight at first; add weight when ready to increase difficulty

7 ONE-ARM ROTATIONAL CABLE ROW

- Stand with pulley machine to left

- Hold pulley attachment in right hand so cord comes across body

- Squat and rotate toward machine with right arm stretched across body

- Drive up and rotate hips and upper body away from machine while pulling right hand across body

- Finish facing away from machine with right arm tucked under ribcage and cord of pulley wrapped around front of hips

COACHING POINTS

- ➡ Focus on rotating hips while standing up out of squat
- ➡ Keep core tight throughout

CARL CRAWFORD'S TRAINING GUIDE

HIP PREHAB

EXERCISE	SETS	REPS
Miniband Walk—Lateral Bent	2	15 each direction
Prone Hip Internal Rotation	2	15
Diagonal Arm Lift—Knees	2	8 each direction
Four-Way Hip Cable	2	10 each direction
Balance	3	30 seconds each leg
Pillar Bridge Front	2	45 seconds
Pillar Bridge Lateral	2	45 seconds each side

MOVEMENT PREP—TURF

EXERCISE	SETS	REPS
Forward Lunge Elbow to Instep	1	10-15 yards
Backward Lunge and Twist	1	10-15 yards
Leg Cradle	1	10-15 yards
Knee Hugs	1	10-15 yards

STRENGTH

EXERCISE	SETS	REPS
Physioball Hanging Knee-Up	3	15
Barbell RDL*	3	5
A-Skip*	3	5 each leg
Split Squat—Foot Up**	3	5 each leg
Reactive Step-Up**	3	5 each leg
Physioball Russian Twist	3	10 each direction
One-Arm Rotational Cable Row	3	5 each direction
* Superset		
** Superset each side		

CHAPTER 2

DERREK LEE

EDITOR'S NOTE

For both STACK and Derrek Lee, 2005 was a special year. For STACK, we launched our company and started publishing the magazine. For Derrek Lee, he had a career season, almost winning the highly coveted but extremely elusive Triple Crown.

Always a talented athlete, Lee had his share of opportunities. Coming out of high school, he had a choice between going straight to the majors and accepting a full ride to play basketball at perennial powerhouse North Carolina. After choosing baseball, Lee quickly found success—and none greater than in 2005, when he clubbed 46 homers, drove in 107 runs, and compiled a league-leading batting average of .335. Although he fell short of the Triple Crown, Lee made his mark as one of Major League Baseball's great players.

That off-season, we set out to find out what fueled Lee's impressive athletic achievements. The Sacramento native was fortunate to have a top training guru right in his backyard, former Sacramento Kings strength coach and industry leader Al Biancani. The fun started each morning at 8:00 a.m., but there was nothing funny about Lee's work ethic. He attacked his workout, clearly

DERREK LEE WATCHES THE FLIGHT OF A HOME RUN IN 2009. LEE HASN'T FORGOTTEN HIS BASKETBALL ROOTS—HIS OFFSEASON WORKOUTS STILL INCLUDE ELEMENTS OF HIS BASKETBALL TRAINING.

demonstrating why he's had such notable success on the diamond. The Chicago Cubs first baseman and team captain graced the cover of *STACK* Magazine's first anniversary issue, and his workout regimen with Biancani was detailed in an exclusive interview. This is the Derrek Lee cover feature as it originally appeared in the February 2006 issue of *STACK* Magazine.

DERREK LEE'S TRIPLE CROWN: DURABILITY, DOMINANCE, DISCIPLINE

In 2003, he took home the World Series Championship with the Florida Marlins and a Gold Glove. The NL batting title and a near miss at the triple crown highlighted his 2005 season with the Chicago Cubs. Lofty accomplishments for All-Star first baseman Derrek Lee, but the list doesn't include the most amazing thing about this super-slugger. In his nine-year major-league career, he's never spent a day on the disabled list.

If you think there's some injury-prevention magic in Lee's hometown of Sacramento, California, you're only half right. It's in Sacramento, but it's not magic. Al Biancani, strength coach and owner of Biancani Fitness, is the power behind Lee's injury-free career.

When most baseball players set their goals for off-season training, they think about what they want to improve on the diamond: a stronger throwing arm, better speed around the bases, quicker feet in the field, more power at the plate. Worthy goals and ambitions? Absolutely. The only benefits to be reaped from dedicated training? Not for Lee and Biancani.

For this duo, time spent training is also about preventing injuries.

"Injury prevention is the number one component of my training plan," Biancani says. "And not only does my plan prevent injuries, but God forbid you do get hurt, you'll come back twice as fast. And I can show you studies that prove it!"

Lee adds, "All the stretching and strength training Al has me do keeps me healthy; it's the greatest thing about his training program. Fortunately, knock on wood, I haven't been on the DL yet."

Why place such a premium on injury prevention? Because mind-blowing speed and the ability to hit the ball a mile are useless when you're sitting in the training room rehabbing a torn hamstring. You need to be on the field to impact the game, and impact player is exactly what Derrek Lee has become.

Biancani's secret to a great training plan is working the whole body. He attacks every area of Lee's body and athleticism by combining weight training with plyometrics, core training,

medicine ball throws, running mechanics, starting techniques, speed ladder drills, and the Shuttle MVP. As a result, Lee has developed the necessary power and explosiveness to dominate the game.

Biancani likens the body to a house. If one part is unstable, the whole house is unstable, which is why the whole body must be trained. The importance of this factor has not gone unnoticed by Lee. "Everything about this workout is good," he says. "It trains every part of my body and works on strength, quickness, explosiveness, everything. It's really hard, and when a workout is hard, you know it's working."

Five days a week during the off-season, Lee gets up in the morning and drives about 45 minutes to train with his longtime coach. "It takes discipline getting up early every day to work out at 8:30 in the morning," Lee says. "Baseball is a long season, so you've got to be mentally disciplined to play your best all season long. That all starts here for me."

We witnessed one of Lee's training sessions last December—a weight workout followed by core, plyometric, Shuttle MVP, box, and med ball circuits. Each element provides specific benefits to Lee's training, and all contribute to keeping the all-star off the DL.

Weight Training

To continually challenge Lee's body and strengthen his muscles, Biancani provides a new stimulus every two weeks by changing rep and set patterns. He splits weight workouts into push and pull days, alternating them through a two-week cycle. With 10 lifting days in each cycle, there are five push and five pull workouts. The reps and sets change after two weeks, but the push-pull split is a constant.

Besides modifying rep and set patterns, Biancani also switches the type of equipment used in workouts. "I like to mix things up between machines, bars, dumbbells and tubing," he says. "All the different pieces of equipment allow me to constantly stress the athlete's body in new ways."

DERREK'S DIRECTIONS

Derrek Lee was a two-sport standout in high school. He signed a letter of intent to play basketball for North Carolina, but followed a path to play baseball after being drafted in the first round by the San Diego Padres. Now entering his 10th season in the big leagues, Lee has learned a thing or two about the world of sports.

Lift in Season.
It helps maintain the work you did in the off-season. Because you remain strong, you don't have to start over when you come back after the season. When you're playing every day, it's easy to slack off and not lift. But now, everyone in the league realizes the importance of lifting. In the past, I slacked off in the second half of the season, my numbers dropped and I felt the difference. Now I always lift throughout the season.

Play More Sports.
The more you play, the better it is for you. Some people say, "If you play baseball, just concentrate on that." I disagree. If you play baseball, basketball and soccer, each sport plays off the others and they work together to make you better. Each sport works on a different part of your game—basketball helps quickness and leg strength, and baseball might improve your hand-eye coordination.

Don't Take Steroids.
There are good reasons why you shouldn't. First, you obviously love the sport you're playing, but is it worth risking your life for it? It's going to negatively affect your health and lifestyle down the road. Second, a question I have for anyone who's an athlete and competitor: don't you want to see how good you are on your own—without cheating? For me, if I had a great season on steroids, I would never know if that was really me doing well.

Enjoy the Game.
There's a lot of pressure on young athletes these days, because they've seen athletes get so much money right out of high school. Scouts—whether they're from the NBA or MLB—come to watch athletes as young as eighth grade, which creates a lot of pressure. I say just enjoy it. Have fun when you're playing, don't let the pressure get to you, and make sure to get that education. That way you'll always have something to fall back on.

WEIGHT WORK

The following weight workout is from a push day in a strength-building rep-set pattern. It consists of sets of 10, 8, 6, and 4 reps.

1 MACHINE INCLINE PRESS

- Lie on back on machine incline press

- Press handles up and away from chest

- Lower handles to starting position

2 BENCH PRESS

- Lie on back on bench

- Place four-inch thick pad on chest near base of breast bone

- Grip bar slightly wider than shoulder width

- Lower bar to pad

- Press bar off pad until arms fully extend

Al's Point: I never do full-range bench. Using the pad removes all stress from the shoulder. The bench is a lift that a lot of athletes like to do, so I don't fight them. I let them do it.

Lee's Point: Because there is no stress on my shoulders, I'm benching more than I ever have.

3 PEC DECK

- Sit upright in pec deck machine with arms apart

- Bring hands and elbows together in front of chest

- Control handles back to starting position

4 DUMBBELL SHRUGS

- Hold dumbbell in each hand with palms facing outside of thighs

- Keeping arms straight, shrug shoulders toward ears

- Lower shoulders to starting position

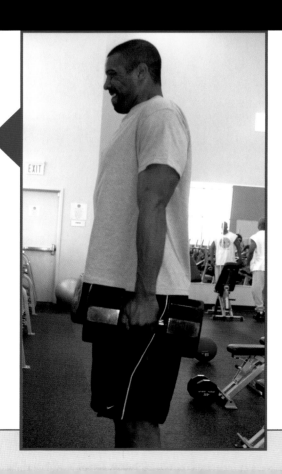

5 LATERAL DUMBBELL RAISE

- Hold dumbbell in each hand with palms facing each other

- With slight bend in elbows, raise arms laterally to shoulder height

- Lower to starting position

6 MACHINE TRICEP PRESS

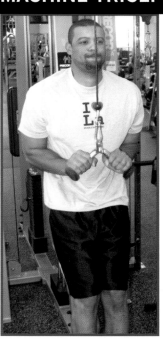

- Stand with back against machine and arms bent

- Hold V attachment with both hands

- Extend arms and press attachment toward thighs keeping elbows tight to sides

- Control back to starting position

MED BALL CORE CIRCUIT

MED BALL SIT-UP

- In sit-up position, hold med ball above head

- Crunch up and touch ball to partner's hands

- Repeat for specified reps

OVERHEAD RUSSIAN TWIST

- In sit-up position, holding med ball above and right of head, crunch up to touch ball to partner's hands

- Lower upper body back to ground and touch ball above and left of head

- Crunch up, touching ball to partner's hands

- Lower upper body back to ground and touch ball above and right of head

- Repeat

RIGHT OVERHEAD TWIST

- In sit-up position holding med ball above and right of head, crunch up and touch ball to partner's hands

- Lower upper body and ball back to starting position

- Repeat

LEFT OVERHEAD TWIST

- Same as right overhead twist, but start with ball to left of head

5 RUSSIAN TWIST

- In sit-up position holding med ball with extended arms to left of stomach, twist right and crunch up to touch ball to partner's hands

- Twist left and sit back to touch ball to left of stomach with arms extended

- Twist right and crunch up to touch ball to partner's hands

- Twist right and sit back to touch ball to right of stomach with arms extended

- Repeat

6 RIGHT RUSSIAN TWIST

- In sit-up position holding med ball with extended arms to right of stomach, twist left and crunch up to touch ball to partner's hands

- Twist right and sit back to touch ball to right of stomach with arms extended

- Repeat

7 LEFT RUSSIAN TWIST

- Same as right Russian twist, but start left and twist right

PLYO CIRCUIT

Before moving on to more advanced and explosive movements, Lee performs a light plyometric circuit to prepare his body and nervous system. "Jumping rope and these other movements are great warm-ups and low-level plyometric activities," Biancani explains. "They're good for working footwork, foot speed, coordination and conditioning."

Perform each movement with only 20–30 seconds rest between.

1 JUMP ROPE

- Continuously jump rope

- Jump with both feet, one foot, or alternating feet

2 SQUAT JUMPS

- Start with feet shoulder width apart

- Lower hips to quarter-squat position

- Jump straight up for maximum height

- Land; immediately repeat

TUCK JUMPS

- Same as squat jumps but tuck knees toward chest during jump

SPLIT LUNGE JUMPS

- Start in lunge position

- Bend knees and lower hips, then jump for maximum height

- Switch leg position in air

- Land; immediately repeat

SHUTTLE MVP CIRCUIT

Although originally created for injury prevention and rehabilitation, the Shuttle MVP has athletic performance benefits for healthy athletes. The machine consists of a padded board that runs along a horizontal track. To add resistance, attach elastic bands to the board.

Lie on your back on the board and place your feet flat against the metal plate. Then, push off the plate in a jumping motion to propel yourself [and the board] along the track against the bands' resistance. Because the landing element is removed, explosive jump training with little or no impact results.

Biancani says, "I was one of the first in the NBA to use the Shuttle MVP, and I've seen great results. It's helped my athletes avoid knee problems as well as increase their verticals."

If you lack access to a Shuttle MVP, Biancani recommends performing the following exercises in a pool.

TWO-LEG JUMPS

- Jump off both legs for maximum distance

- Repeat jumps as fast as possible

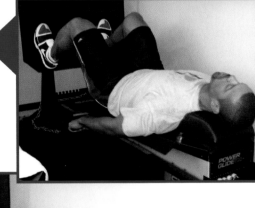

2 SINGLE-LEG JUMPS

- Jump off one leg for maximum distance

- Repeat jumps on same leg as fast as possible

- Repeat with opposite leg

3 ALTERNATING SINGLE-LEG JUMPS

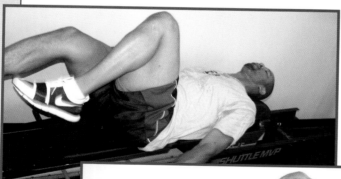

- Jump off one leg for maximum distance

- Land on opposite leg and jump again for maximum distance

- Repeat

PLYO BOX CIRCUIT

Plyometrics with a 12-inch box is the next progression of explosive movements—introduced only after the body is prepared from working on the Shuttle MVP.

"We'll work Derrek on the Shuttle MVP until he can handle about 400 touches," Biancani says. "He gradually works to where he's doing some Shuttle and some box work. And by the time he leaves for spring training, he'll be doing all box work."

Perform the following movements in rapid succession with only 20–30 seconds of rest between.

1 LATERAL ONE UP, ONE DOWN

- Start with left foot on ground to left of box and right foot on top of box

- Jump up and right

- Land with right foot on ground and left foot on box

- Jump up and left

- Land with left foot on ground and right foot on box

- Repeat

2 RIGHT FOOT LATERAL STEP-UPS

- Start with left foot on ground to left of box and right foot on top of box

- Jump off right foot for maximum height

- Land in starting position and immediately jump again

3 LEFT FOOT LATERAL STEP-UPS

- Same as Right Foot Lateral Step-Ups, but with right foot on ground and left foot on box

4 ALTERNATING STEP-UPS

- Start with left foot on ground behind box and right foot on top of box

- Jump off right foot for maximum height

- Switch leg position in air and land with right foot on ground and left foot on box

- Jump off left foot for maximum height

- Switch legs in air and land in original starting position

- Repeat

- Start with feet together on ground to left of box

- Jump right onto box for speed

- Jump for speed onto ground to right of box

- Immediately jump left onto box for speed

- Jump for speed onto ground to left of box

- Repeat

MED BALL THROW CIRCUIT

"Medicine ball throws are upper body plyo drills," Biancani explains. "Because rotational movements are so prevalent in baseball, we use a lot of them to train. These throws really work the core."

The first four movements are performed on a core board, which provides an unstable surface. The board swivels and rocks, making the athlete overcome forces from all directions and maintain balance.

"Hitting is all about balance, which is when these drills come into play," Biancani says.

Perform the following drills in rapid succession with 20–30 seconds rest between movements.

1 CHEST PASS

- Stand on core board facing partner 10–15 feet away

- Hold med ball at chest with both hands

- Push ball away from chest and throw to partner

- Catch pass from partner

- Repeat

OVERHEAD PASS

- Stand on core board facing partner 10–15 feet away

- Hold med ball with both hands above and behind head

- Throw ball overhead to partner

- Catch pass from partner

- Repeat

BACKWARD OVERHEAD PASS

- Stand with feet shoulder-width apart in quarter-squat position

- Hold med ball at chest with both hands

- Extending at ankles, knees, and hips, throw ball backward over head toward ground

- Target throw to land 8–10 feet behind you

- Stand on core board with left shoulder facing partner 10–15 feet away

- Hold med ball with both hands and rotate right, away from partner

- Rotate back toward partner and throw ball to him

- Catch pass from partner

- Repeat

5 SIDE THROWS [RIGHT]

- Same as side throws [left] but stand with right shoulder facing partner and rotate left

FLEXIBILITY

Improving range of motion is a cornerstone of Biancani's training plan. Over the course of a workout, Lee stretches up to three times. Of particular importance is stretching before and after workouts. Although many coaches have moved away from static stretches prior to activity, Biancani thinks static stretching combined with dynamic movements produces the best warm-up.

"A lot of people are black and white when it comes to static and dynamic stretching. There's a war of words going on right now about which is better for a warm-up," he says. "I believe there are shades of grey on this issue, so I use a combination of both."

Perform the following stretches with a partner. Hold each stretch for 10–15 seconds.

1 KNEE TO CHEST

- Lie on back

- Bring one knee to chest

- Partner pushes foot toward opposite hip and knee toward chest

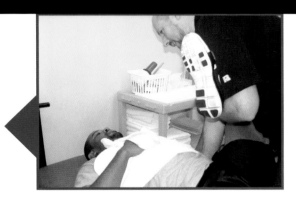

2 HIP FLEXOR AND QUAD STRETCH

- Lie on stomach

- Bend knee and bring foot toward glute

- Partner pulls up on thigh to lift off table or ground

3 IT BAND STRETCH

- Lie on back

- Bend knee of one leg and cross over opposite leg

- Partner pushes thigh of bent leg toward table or ground

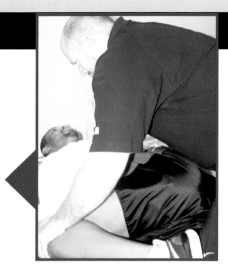

4 HAMSTRING STRETCH

- Lie on back

- Keeping leg straight, bring foot toward head

- Partner pushes leg toward head, holds leg straight

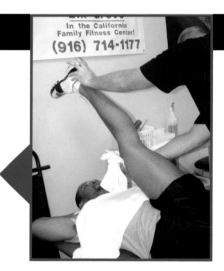

5 GROIN STRETCH

- Lie on back

- Bend knee of one leg and place foot on thigh of opposite leg

- Partner pushes knee toward table or ground

DERREK LEE'S TRAINING GUIDE

WEIGHT WORK

EXERCISE	SETS/REPS
Machine Incline Press	1x10, 1x8, 1x6, 1x4
Bench Press	1x10, 1x8, 1x6, 1x4
Pec Deck	1x10, 1x8, 1x6, 1x4
DB Shrugs	3x6
Lateral DB Raise	1x10, 1x8, 1x6, 1x4
Machine Tricep Press	1x10, 1x8, 1x6, 1x4

MED BALL CIRCUIT

EXERCISE	SETS/REPS
Med Ball Sit-Up	1x30
Overhead Russian Twist	1x30
Right Overhead Twist	1x15
Left Overhead Twist	1x15
Russian Twist	1x30
Right Russian Twist	1x15
Left Russian Twist	1x15
Med Ball Crunches	1x30

PLYO CIRCUIT

EXERCISE	SETS/REPS
Jump Rope	1x60 seconds
Squat Jumps	1x30
Jump Rope	1x60 seconds
Tuck Jumps	1x30
Jump Rope	1x60 seconds
Split/Lunge Jumps	1x15 each side

SHUTTLE MVP CIRCUIT

EXERCISE	SETS/REPS
Two-Leg Jumps	1x30
Single-Leg Jumps [R,L]	1x15 each direction
Two-Leg Jumps	1x30
Alternating Single-Leg Jumps	1x15 each side
Two-Leg Jumps	1x30
Single-Leg Jumps [R,L]	1x15 each direction
Two-Leg Jumps	1x30

PLYO BOX CIRCUIT

EXERCISE	SETS/REPS
Lateral One Up, One Down	1x30
Lateral Step-Ups [R,L]	1x15 each direction
Alternating Step-Ups	1x30
Two-Leg Lateral Jumps	1x30

MED BALL THROW CIRCUIT

EXERCISE	SETS/REPS
Chest Pass	1x30
Overhead Pass	1x30
Backward Overhead Pass	1x30
Side Throws [R,L]	1x30 each direction

CHAPTER 3

DUSTIN PEDROIA

EDITOR'S NOTE

Athletes' Performance graciously opened its facility in Tempe, Arizona, to STACK in February 2008 for a training and photo shoot with Boston Red Sox electrifying second baseman Dustin Pedroia. Despite his smaller [5'9", 180-pound] frame, from the moment he started to train, Pedroia exemplified the perfect STACK athlete.

AP's director of methodology, Craig Friedman, put Pedroia through a workout that included medicine ball work for rotational power, upper-body strength and power training, and lower-body explosive power work. Throughout the session, Pedroia demonstrated his incredible work ethic, as he attacked every exercise with a no-nonsense approach and impeccable attention to detail.

Watching Pedroia orchestrate Boston's infield reveals his leadership skills. What's impressive, though, is how he uses those same qualities in the weight room. As he sweated through Friedman's workout with other major league players, the superstar was first to perform each exercise and offered encouragement to his peers with each rep.

Thanks to Friedman's off-season program and Pedroia's dedication and athleticism, it's safe

DUSTIN PEDROIA WATCHES A DRIVE IN A 2009 GAME. DESPITE HIS SMALL STATURE, PEDROIA GENERATES GREAT ROTATIONAL POWER IN HIS SWING.

to assume that this young man will be adding more hardware to his growing collection. In 2007, he won a World Series ring and the AL Rookie of the Year award with a .317 average, eight homers and 50 RBIs. He followed that up with an AL MVP season, going .326 at the plate with 17 long balls and a clutch 83 RBIs to join Cal Ripken, Jr. and Ryan Howard as the only players in MLB history to win Rookie of the Year and Most Valuable Player in consecutive seasons.

This is the Dustin Pedroia cover feature as it originally appeared in the March 2009 issue of *STACK* Magazine.

DUSTIN' THE COMPETITION

While most baseball fans were probably shocked that a man measuring just 5'9" and weighing 180 pounds had won Major League Baseball's most coveted individual accolade, we at STACK weren't the least bit surprised. Dustin Pedroia personifies what hard work can do for athletes of any size and shape. His unyielding work ethic helped him hoist the 2008 AL Most Valuable Player trophy while leading the Boston Red Sox to the seventh game of the American League Championship Series.

Though he's only been on the MLB scene for two years, Pedroia plays the game like a grizzled veteran. He has already accomplished more than most do in a career. In 2007, the gritty second baseman earned a World Series ring and was named the AL Rookie of the Year.

"When I first got called up to the major leagues in 2006, I really didn't know what to expect," Pedroia says. "I really didn't set any expectations or goals on myself. My biggest thing was, if I'm in the lineup that day, I'm going to play as hard as I can and try to help our team.

That's been my mentality ever since I got called up. That's how I'm going to be successful. I have to keep that mindset every season. This year, I was very successful. Hopefully, I can continue that."

Because of his win-at-all-costs attitude, individual awards have followed Pedroia at every level of his baseball career—even though he admits that personal honors aren't something he sets his sights on. But despite the successes and the fact that he dominated the high school landscape in Woodland, California, college coaches and pro scouts steered away because of his minuscule 5'2" and 140-pound frame. It wasn't until his senior season, when he destroyed opposing pitchers at California's Area Code Games, that college offers came rolling in.

Pedroia chose Arizona State University, one of the more prestigious programs in the country. "I had four other trips planned out, [but] I wanted to play in the PAC-10, so I cancelled all my trips and kind of committed [to ASU]," he says. "I knew if I went there, I would have a good chance of getting drafted and playing professional baseball."

With a goal in mind and a burning desire to make it a reality, Pedroia dominated his college experience while molding a baseball resume highlighted by talent, unselfish play, and a workout regimen that is still with him today.

A Star in the Desert

Pedroia wasted little time showing that he belonged at a top-tier college program. His stellar freshman campaign helped him grab second-team all-conference honors. A gifted athlete with solid natural hitting instincts, he also was improving in the field, morphing from a good defensive player into a great one.

Then, proving that his team-first mentality wasn't all talk, Pedroia gave up his scholarship prior to his sophomore year so the team could sign a stud pitcher. That season, that former JUCO hurler went undefeated with a 2.73 ERA, while Pedroia was the PAC-10 Co-Player of the Year and Second-Team All-American, helping the Sun Devils reach the NCAA Regionals.

He topped that by earning a First-Team All-American nod his final season. "I was on pretty much a full ride, so I gave it back so we could get this guy," he says. "I got drafted pretty high, so I figured if I gave my scholarship back I'd be able to have enough money in the long run anyway. So it's one of those things that I had to do for that guy."

"Once you get to college, they have people who prepare you [for success]," he says. "In the fall, when we weren't playing, [the goal was] get as strong as you can and as fast as you can; I try to take that into professional baseball, as well." During his three years at ASU, Pedroia began to realize how a strict training regimen could positively influence his game. Blend that with a five-inch growth spurt—and an abundance of natural athletic ability—and you get a rock-solid baseball foundation.

With all the essentials in tow, Pedroia embarked on his MLB dream when the Boston Red Sox chose him in the second round of the 2004 draft. It didn't take long for him to make an impact. He dominated minor-league hurlers and was an every-day big leaguer by the start of the 2007 season.

Baseball enthusiasts often identify Pedroia as Boston's mighty-mite second baseman, but to his peers, he's one of the most dedicated and intense players in the game. "I'm not the biggest guy in the world, so you always have those doubters that say you're too small and you can't do this, or you can't do that," he says. "But you have to go out there and prove them wrong every day."

Off-Season Training

To prove the naysayers wrong—and to make sure they pay more attention to his talent than to his size—Pedroia has amped up his winter training. He spends his off-season in a familiar locale, at Athletes' Performance in Tempe, Arizona. At the state-of-the-art facility, which is a stone's throw away from ASU's athletic facilities, Pedroia receives top-of-the-line training from Craig Friedman, AP's director of methodology.

According to Friedman, Pedroia brings a nonstop motor and an impeccable work ethic every time he steps foot on AP's grounds. "He

knows that if all he does is show up, that's not going to be enough, and he definitely brings his work ethic anytime he comes to the field and anytime he comes to a workout," Friedman says. "Dustin is an extremely hardworking athlete, and at the same time very confident. I think that confidence comes from his hard work, because he is probably considered a undersized, underpowered athlete, and I think he has to work harder than most athletes to be able to do what he needs to do on the field."

Pedroia has had to increase his training to stay fit throughout the marathon MLB season, with an emphasis on getting stronger and faster. The more-intense workouts also have been key to unlocking and maintaining his elite-athlete status. "That's why I train [at AP] and get ready for the season, because I feel it's the best fit for me and makes me become a better athlete," he says. "I'm just trying to get faster and stronger. Last off-season, I had surgery on my hand, so it kind of affected me a little bit in getting stronger. This off-season I was healthy, and I was able to get a lot stronger and a lot faster."

Since baseball involves so much rotation and upper-body strength, Friedman runs Pedroia through sport-specific exercises that help him get stronger and stay injury-free. "Playing the game of baseball at a high level puts your body in awkward positions and involves a lot of rotation, so we try to mimic those movements during workouts to simulate game-type situations," Friedman says.

Rookie of the Year, MVP, and World Series champ in just two years could make some athletes complacent. But Pedroia isn't just any athlete—he's a standout on the cusp of superstardom thanks to his all-business approach to the weight room and diamond.

Too small to be a star? Where are those naysayers now?

MEDICINE BALL ROTATIONAL POWER

Friedman: "The rotational emphasis is working on the kinetic chain, which passes power through the body from the hips and feet, up through the torso and arms. You have to let the hips be the trigger and let the torso be the conduit to get everything going through your hands and into the medicine ball."

Perform the following med ball exercises standing three to four feet away from a wall.

PARALLEL THROWS

- Holding med ball in front, assume athletic stance facing a wall with feet slightly wider than shoulder width

- Rotate left until med ball is at left hip

- Leading with hips, explosively rotate right to throw ball against wall as hard as possible

- Catch rebound; repeat for specified reps

- Perform set on opposite side

COACHING POINTS

➤ Keep weight evenly distributed
➤ Make sure to initiate throw with back hip
➤ Throw med ball with hips more than arms

- Holding med ball in front, assume athletic stance with feet slightly wider than shoulder width and wall to right

- Rotate left until med ball is behind left hip

- Leading with hips, explosively rotate right to throw ball against wall as hard as possible

- Catch rebound; repeat for specified reps

- Perform set on opposite side

COACHING POINTS

- ➡ Keep back flat and chest up
- ➡ Make sure to initiate throw with back hip
- ➡ Throw ball against wall so you can catch it in same path you threw it

3 ROTATIONAL CHEST PASS

- Holding med ball in front of chest, assume athletic stance with feet slightly wider than shoulder width and wall to right

- Leading with hips, explosively rotate right and fully extend back arm to push ball against wall as hard as possible

- Catch rebound; repeat for specified reps

- Perform set on opposite side

COACHING POINTS

4 ROTATIONAL SLAMS

- Holding med ball at waist level, assume athletic stance with feet slightly wider than shoulder width

- Using hips and torso, swing ball right and then overhead in circular motion

- Explosively throw med ball into ground in front of right foot

- Catch rebound; repeat for specified reps

- Perform set on opposite side

COACHING POINTS

➤ Reach ball as high as possible over head, without extending backward

➤ Explosively throw ball to ground by contracting abs, upper back muscles and arms

➤ Keep hips tall during throw with core tight and back flat

UPPER-BODY STRENGTH AND POWER

Friedman: "With so much throwing and rotating in baseball, it's important to strengthen your upper body to prevent injury. Two of the exercises we perform really help build strength in the necessary areas. The Rotational Row really teaches you how to transfer power from your legs through your torso and into your arms. The X Pull Down strengthens your entire posterior chain, protecting your shoulders from injury. The Weighted Neutral-Grip Pull-Up really works grip, back and core strength."

ROTATIONAL ROW

- With cable machine to right, assume athletic stance with feet slightly wider than shoulder width

- Reach across body with left hand, turning hips and shoulders to cable machine, to hold handle set at low position

- Explosively rotate hips left and bring handle across body until it's tucked under left armpit

- Return to start position; repeat for specified reps

- Perform set on opposite side

COACHING POINTS

➥ Turn shoulders toward and away from cable machine with each rep

➥ Make sure hips are pointed away from weight stack at end of each rep

➥ Movement should feel like a rotational clean pull

2 X PULL DOWN

- Kneel in front of crossover cable machine; cross arms and grasp opposite handles with hands

- Without arching back, retract shoulder blades, then pull elbows to side of body; straighten and externally rotate arms in fluid motion so thumbs point back

- Return to start position; repeat for specified reps

COACHING POINTS

- Use shoulder blades, not arms, to initiate movement
- Keep stomach tight, chest up, and head straight throughout movement
- Get chest as big as possible in finished position

3 WEIGHTED NEUTRAL-GRIP PULL-UP

- With weight attached to belt around waist, grab neutral-grip pull-up handles so palms face each other

- Pull yourself up until chin is above bar

- Lower with control until arms are almost straight

- Repeat for specified reps

COACHING POINTS

- Perform movement while staying as vertical as possible to avoid turning it into a horizontal pull
- Keep back straight and don't use body for momentum
- Keep slight bend in elbows at bottom of pull-up

LOWER BODY EXPLOSIVE POWER

Friedman: "We'll perform Squat Jumps immediately following our primary lower-body strength movement for that day. The Squat Jump really helps with explosive power and speed."

1 SQUAT JUMP

- Begin with feet slightly wider than shoulder width and hands behind head

- Perform squat, then explosively jump as high as possible

- Land softly in squat position; immediately perform again

- Repeat for specified reps

COACHING POINTS

- Don't let knees go beyond toes in squat position
- Jump into full extension and try to pull toes to shins in mid-air
- Keep chest up and fully extend hips during jump
- Absorb landing through hips rather than knees

DUSTIN PEDROIA'S TRAINING GUIDE

MEDICINE BALL ROTATIONAL POWER

EXERCISE	SETS/REPS
Parallel Throws	2x5 each side
Perpendicular Throws	2x5 each side
Rotational Chest Pass	2x5 each side
Rotational Slams	2x5 each side

UPPER-BODY STRENGTH AND POWER

EXERCISE	SETS/REPS
Rotational Row	2x10 each side
X Pull Down	2x10
Weighted Neutral-Grip Pull-Up	3x8

LOWER-BODY EXPLOSION POWER

EXERCISE	SETS/REPS
Squat Jump	3x8

CHAPTER **4**

ERIC CHAVEZ

EDITOR'S NOTE

Eric Chavez, who has taken home a Silver Slugger and six Gold Glove Awards, is a hard-working player with a blue-collar approach to the game. As if these were not sufficient credentials for a *STACK* cover, we approached Chavez at a time when many prominent baseball players were either complaining about their compensation or being implicated for using performance-enhancing drugs. Chavez was a breath of fresh air and a ray of hope for the game of baseball.

A final factor in our decision to feature the Oakland A's slugger was his dedication to training at one of the world's top facilities, Athletes' Performance in Tempe, Arizona, with one of the industry's most respected experts, AP founder and chairman Mark Verstegen. Before AP, Chavez had subscribed to the old-school style of lifting—heavy sets—which had him leaving the gym with a massive pump and tight shoulders, but with little improvement to his athleticism or baseball ability.

Training at AP helped Chavez focus on the full-body movement patterns he would use on the diamond, whether swinging a bat or chasing down balls hit in the hole. Verstegen prescribed

ERIC CHAVEZ FOLLOWS THROUGH ON A SWING DURING A SPRING TRAINING GAME IN 2009. PREHAB TRAINING HAS HELPED CHAVEZ PROTECT HIS JOINTS FROM OVERUSE INJURIES, WHICH ARE COMMON IN BASEBALL.

specific prehab exercises that set out to strengthen the small muscles around Chavez's joints to protect them from overuse injuries.

Although he worked hard to protect his body, Chavez was ravaged by physical problems that no type of training can prevent—herniated discs—which initially put his career in jeopardy. But after two back surgeries, the veteran third baseman is feeling better than expected and plans to be ready for spring training in 2010.

This is the Eric Chavez cover feature as it appeared in the April 2006 issue of *STACK* Magazine.

PRIDE AND POWER

Some blame the era of "big business baseball." Others point to overpaid sluggers who refuse to dig out ground balls. Maybe it's the spoiled millionaires who show up to spring training either unprepared or with suspiciously large biceps. Whatever it is, the passion, love, and support for America's pastime have been damaged.

A few overexposed problems and athletes have overshadowed the fact that most players still bust their butts to remain on top. Because despite what cynics believe, the major league off-season is not about arbitration, questionable supplements, and salary disputes. It's about old-fashioned preparation—players working to get their minds right and bodies ready for the upcoming season.

If you're a fan who's turned your back on the game, prepare to fall in love again. You will undoubtedly find solace— and a new faith in baseball—after studying Eric Chavez's dedication and work habits. The will of this man isn't rooted in a desire for recognition. It's not about the paper. It's about his pride in and loyalty to the equally dedicated men who don the Oakland uniform alongside him.

The game welcomes you back—no hard feelings.

"Part of being an athlete in any sport is having pride—regardless of the situation. And that goes all the way down to your preparation," Chavez says. "You owe it to yourself—and the team that has put faith in you— to always work to get better. In the off-season, do everything in your power to improve physically."

Every off-season, energized with this fortitude and pride, Chavez heads to Athletes' Performance Institute in Tempe, Arizona.

to train with performance specialist Mark Verstegen. Chavez's dedication to training quickly became clear to Verstegen: "Eric loves being able perform at his best—and his results speak for themselves. He exemplifies what an athlete can do to maximize his career."

Chavez reciprocates the respect. "API's training is something special," he says. "They've gotten me away from traditional weightlifting— walking into the gym, lifting heavy and leaving all [swollen]. In this program, everything we

do—every stretch, exercise, and drill—has a purpose and incorporates what I do on the baseball field."

API's comprehensive program aims to supply Chavez with every tool he needs to exploit his baseball ability. "We want to keep Eric's range at a world-class level and improve his time from home to first. We also want to optimize his power output pound for pound—rotationally and linearly," Verstegen says. "This relative power is what baseball is all about."

Improving Chavez's already-sick game comes from what Verstegen calls "the rubber-band effect." "We first work on Eric's stability—you can't store or release energy without stability," Verstegen says. "After that, we work on mobility to bring the energy into the muscle, and improve elasticity and power to increase his range, arm speed and ability to drive the ball harder."

Chavez says API has helped him generate a "snap" and power different from any other training he has experienced. "That's why I keep coming back," he explains. "After my first year here, I could generate so much more power at the plate. The exercises that help me create that quick snap and rotational power are great for me. Baseball is a game of fractions of seconds, and generating power within those fractions is what I try to do. That's what separates the best."

Beyond improving Chavez's offensive power and defensive movements, API works toward preventing shoulder injuries, which are common among big leaguers. Verstegen says, "The training protects Eric's body against the natural wear and tear of the game." At the end of last season, Chavez was experiencing problems with his throwing shoulder. Instead of surgery, he returned to API, entrusting his shoulder to Verstegen's program. He says, "They really focus on rotator cuff work and exercises to strengthen the little muscles in there, and avoid lifting heavy weights overhead."

The 12th man in history to hit 30 home runs in a Gold Glove-winning season, Chavez has returned to his off-season training hungrier than ever. He says, "I want my power numbers to be up—I am shooting for career highs in RBI and home runs this year. I'm dedicating myself to this workout process, because I think this is going to be a big year for our organization— one of those years when everything comes together."

If dedication and pride define you the way they do Eric Chavez, get ready for your own career-best season.

Long Ball

Calling Major League Baseball players "the boys of summer" isn't entirely correct. When the pre- and post-seasons are counted, these athletes are competing most of the year. And although your school's season is much shorter, playing in summer leagues and on traveling teams takes a toll on your body.

Consistency, a positive attitude and the ability to focus determine success as much as physical strength and skill. "The mental part of baseball is undoubtedly the toughest part," Chavez says. "We are out there six times a week with only two to three days off a month over a six-month period. No other sport compares."

Chavez has established a method to remain fresh throughout the long season. He says: "When things start going badly, you start to question yourself. That's when I have to remind myself that I can do it, I'm talented, and I'm here for a reason."

API's training also helps. "Something about this training sticks with me throughout the whole season," Chavez says. "It was always tough to maintain strength and power for so long with such a busy game schedule. But all the improvements in strength and quickness that I make in the off-season stay with me. I love knowing my hard work will last me that long."

To rejuvenate his body from the grind of hard-hit groundballs and life on the base paths, Chavez uses hot and cold contrast baths. "Every day during the season, I hop in the cold tank to help me get rid of all the aches and pains," he says. "I get there early, sit in the cold water, and then hop in the hot tank for two minutes to warm my body up again. It's like recharging the batteries each day, and I feel huge recovery benefits from it. It's tough. Most guys go up to their waists, but I go full-body."

The cold dunk isn't limited to the season. Verstegen says, "The contrast baths are great for recovery and regeneration. Our philosophy is that work plus rest equals success. We work hard, and then recover to let the training effects set in."

PREHAB

Verstegen estimates that 65 to 70 percent of baseball injuries result from overuse. "Our prehab is a proactive way to head off the most common sports injuries pro athletes experience from overuse," he says. "We set out to protect Eric's body on a fundamental level by making sure his mobility and stability are clean in efficient movement patterns." Only after the fundamentals are established, Verstegen & Co. work on building Eric's performance.

TENNIS BALL THORACIC MOBS

Targeted Muscles: Mid back

- Tape two tennis balls together to form peanut shape

- Lie on back; position tennis balls vertically under thoracic spine (mid to upper back)

- Bend knees 90 degrees

- Hold arms straight above chest pointing to ceiling

- Without arching lower back, lower one arm until it's overhead, then move arm back to start position

- Repeat with opposite arm and continue alternating for specified reps

- Move balls up spine 1–2 inches each set

COACHING POINTS

➧ Go through full range of motion

➧ Keep head in neutral position

➧ Avoid any unnecessary movement with body

2 SHOULDER EXTERNAL ROTATION AT 30 DEGREES

Targeted muscles: Rotator cuff, back of shoulder

- Stand with shoulders perpendicular to cable machine

- Make sure chest is up, abs are drawn in

- Hold handle with outside hand, then bend that arm 90 degrees, keeping elbow four inches from ribs

- Rotate hand outward

- Return to start position with control

- Repeat for specified reps

- Perform set on opposite side

COACHING POINTS

- Make sure chest is up and abs are drawn in
- Avoid moving elbow or rotating body during exercise
- Go through full range of motion

STRENGTH WORK

PULL-UP [NEUTRAL GRIP]

Targeted muscles: Back, shoulders, biceps

Verstegen: "Pull-ups are one of the best scapular exercises you can do if you have healthy shoulders. We first use Keiser machines for assistance and gradually work toward using them for resistance. The neutral grip frees up the motion and decreases the chance of shoulder or elbow impingement.

- Assume neutral grip [palms facing each other] on pull-up bar

- Pull body up until chin is above bar

- Lower with control

- Repeat for specified reps

COACHING POINTS

➡ Perform movement while staying as vertical as possible to avoid turning it into horizontal pull

➡ Keep back straight and don't use body for momentum

2 MEDICINE BALL LINEAR CHOP

Targeted muscles: Back, shoulders, abs

- Assume athletic stance with feet shoulder-width apart holding med ball in front

- Raise med ball back and overhead

- Chop down with arms and abs to throw med ball to ground

- Repeat for specified reps

COACHING POINTS

- ➡ Keep core tight throughout movement
- ➡ Throw med ball into ground as hard as possible
- ➡ Come up onto toes while taking med ball back and overhead

3 HEEL SIT MID-THORACIC STRETCH

Targeted muscles: Mid-back

Verstegen: "We want Eric's lumbar spine [lower back] to be stable and his thoracic spine [mid back] mobile. This exercise mobilizes and then activates that region, so he learns to transfer force. This improves his throwing ability and rotational power. We've tried to teach Eric to capture the energy of his hips so he can release better through his pillar, out of his hand or through his bat. This helps because his whole torso sits on top of his hips, and it decreases stress on his lower and mid back."

- Sit with knees on ground, butt on heels, stomach on upper thighs, left arm extended forward with hand on ground, and right hand behind head

- Keeping stomach on thighs, open chest to right and hold for two seconds

- Return to start position; repeat for specified reps

- Perform set on opposite side

COACHING POINTS

- ➡ Don't allow hips to rise
- ➡ Keep back as straight as possible
- ➡ Open chest as much as possible
- ➡ Keep hand, feet, and knees on ground throughout exercise

4 LATERAL HALF-KNEEL CABLE CHOP

Targeted muscles: Hips, shoulders, triceps, abs

Verstegen: "This helps Eric generate maximum power in the specific muscles he uses for baseball movements. It also works his core and improves his hips' ability to stabilize and rotate."

- Position body perpendicular to cable machine with outside knee on ground

- Hold handle from high cable position with both hands

- Rotate shoulders toward machine, then pull handle to chest as you rotate away

- In continuous motion continue pushing handle down and away

- Return to start position; repeat for specified reps

- Perform set on opposite side

COACHING POINTS

- ➡ Keep back straight and head in neutral position throughout exercise
- ➡ Go through full range of motion
- ➡ Finish with chest up, shoulder blades back and down and stomach tight

5 SINGLE-ARM SPEED CHOP

Targeted muscles: Hips, shoulder, triceps, abs

Verstegen: "This also improves power output and helps the hips and core stabilize and rotate."

- Position body perpendicular to cable machine with outside knee on ground

- Hold handle from high cable position with outside hand

- Rotate shoulders toward machine, then rotate away

- In continuous motion pull handle across body and down in chopping motion

- Return to start position; repeat for specified reps

- Perform set on opposite side

COACHING POINTS

- ➡ Keep back straight and head in neutral position throughout exercise
- ➡ Go through full range of motion
- ➡ Finish with core tight and chest up

6 DOWEL SHOULDER STRETCH

Targeted muscles: Shoulders, upper back

Verstegen: "This opens Eric's shoulders to improve mobility."

- Hold dowel in front—right palm facing up, left palm facing down

- Keeping arms straight, rotate right hand toward left until right palm faces ground

- When you feel slight stretch in back of right shoulder, return to start position

- Repeat for specified reps

- Switch position of hands; repeat in opposite direction

COACHING POINTS

➥ Keep back straight and head in neutral position throughout exercise

7 DUMBBELL PULLOVER—EXTENSION

Targeted muscles: Back, triceps

- Lie on back on bench holding dumbbells with arms extended over chest and shoulders

- Bend arms 90 degrees without allowing elbows to splay out

- Maintaining 90-degree bend in elbows, lower weights toward floor as far as possible without discomfort

- Drive elbows to start position and straighten arms in one motion

- Repeat for specified reps

COACHING POINTS

➥ Go through full range of motion
➥ Keep back flat on bench and head in neutral position throughout exercise
➥ Avoid using body for momentum

SINGLE-ARM, SINGLE-LEG DUMBBELL ROW

Targeted muscles: Lats, rear delts, glutes, hips

Verstegen: "This is the ultimate lift to get that cross-action across the back of your body. We look for stability across the hips, glutes, and lower back, all the way up to the lats. It's the same action used when you run."

- Holding dumbbell in left hand, stand with slight bend in right leg, then hinge over at waist

- Place right hand on stable, waist-high surface

- Lift left leg to form "T" with body

- Slide left shoulder blade toward spine, then lift weight toward body by driving elbow toward ceiling,

- Return to start position with control; repeat for specified reps

- Perform set on opposite side

COACHING POINTS

- ➡ Make sure to fire glute on raised leg in "T" position
- ➡ Keep back flat, head in neutral position, and core tight throughout exercise
- ➡ Keep elbow tight to ribs during row portion of exercise

PHYSIOBALL/FLOOR Y, T, W, L

9

Targeted muscles: Rotator cuffs, shoulders, upper back

Verstegen: "This is part of our pillar strength series. We want to ensure everything works together. So our cuff work integrates pillar strength by working the shoulders, torso and hips together"

Y

- Lie with stomach on physioball

- With thumbs up and arms straight, raise arms in front so body and arms form "Y"

- Repeat for specified reps

T

- Lie with stomach on floor

- With thumbs up and arms straight, raise arms to side so body and arms form "T"

- Repeat for specified reps

W

- Lie with stomach on physioball

- With thumbs up, arms bent, and elbows tight to ribcage, squeeze shoulder blades down and rotate hands as far back as possible so arms form "W"

- Repeat for specified reps

L

- Lie with stomach on physioball

- With arms hanging toward floor, make 90-degree angle with elbows and bend arms so upper arms are parallel to floor

- Externally rotate upper arms so backs of hands rotate toward ceiling

- Repeat for specified reps

COACHING POINTS

POWER PLATE PUSH-UP (30 HZ)

Targeted muscles: Chest, shoulders, arms, abs

Verstegen: "The PowerPlate improves mobility, stability and elasticity. Our guys have had great results using it before upper-body work, or before squatting actions. They feel more stable, powerful and activated after using it. It serves both prehab and performance enhancement purposes."

- Assume push-up position on Power Plate

- Lower chest to Power Plate

- Return to start position

- Repeat for specified reps with machine at 30 Hz

COACHING POINTS

➡ Keep back flat and head in neutral position
➡ Go through full range of motion

ERIC CHAVEZ'S TRAINING GUIDE

PREHAB

EXERCISE	SETS/REPS
Tennis Ball Thoracic MOBS	2x8 each arm
Shoulder External Rotation	1x20 each arm
Miniband Walk—Linear	2x15 steps

MOVEMENT PREP

EXERCISE	SETS/DISTANCE [YARDS]
Forward Lunge—Forearm to Instep	2 x 15-20
Backward Lunge With Twist	2 x 15-20
Walking Knee Hugs	2 x 15-20
Inverted Hamstring	2 x 15-20
Hand Walk	2 x 15-20

PLYOS

EXERCISE	SETS/REPS
45-Degree Bound—Hold/Quick*	2x4 each leg
Medial Lateral Hurdle Hop	2x4 each leg
Hurdle Jump—Continuous	2x6
Box Blast—Alternating Continuous	2x6 each leg

* Perform Hold variation first; then progress to Quick

MOVEMENT

EXERCISE	SETS/DISTANCE [YARDS]
Ankling	3x20
Heel Slide Run	2x20
Step-Over Run	2x20
Build-Up	3x60

MEDICINE BALL ROUTINE

EXERCISE	SETS/REPS
Parallel/Perpendicular Single-Leg Rotational Throw	1x6 each side
Parallel/Perpendicular Contrast Throw	2x10 + 5 each side
Reverse Throw	2x10 each side
Squat to Press Throw—Contrast	2x5 + 3

STRENGTH

EXERCISE	SETS/REPS
Pull-Up (Neutral Grip)*	1x4, 3x3
Med Ball Linear Chop*	3x4
Standing Chest Stretch	1x3 each side
Dumbbell Incline Bench	1x4, 3x3
Heel Sit Mid-Thoracic Stretch	1x6 each side
Lateral Half-Kneel Cable Chop**	3x4 each side
Single-Arm Speed Chop**	3x6 each side
Dowel Shoulder Stretch	2x6 each side
Dumbbell Pullover-Extension	2x6
Single-Arm, Single-Leg Dumbbell Row	2x6 each side
X Pulldown	2x6
EZ Curl	2x6
PowerPlate Push-up	2x15
Forearm Circuit	
Supine Lat Stretch	1x6

* Superset
** Superset each side

CHAPTER 5

JEFF FRANCOEUR

EDITOR'S NOTE

After Jeff Francoeur's stellar rookie campaign in 2005—he finished third in the balloting for NL Rookie of the Year despite playing only half a season—we traveled down to his high school alma mater in Lilburn, Georgia, to catch up with the dual-sport hometown hero. Although he was busy filming a commercial, chatting it up with current high school athletes and coaches, and grabbing a workout, "Frenchy" graciously allotted some time to speak with us about his impressive athletic résumé.

An exceptional athlete at Parkview High School, the man affectionately dubbed "The Natural" led his football and baseball teams to two consecutive state championships. One of Georgia's most heavily pursued and recruited athletes, Francoeur turned down a football scholarship at Clemson after being selected in the first round of the 2002 Major League Baseball Draft by his hometown Atlanta Braves. Facing tremendous Peach State pressure, Francoeur nevertheless skyrocketed up through the Braves farm system to reach the big leagues in July 2005, and then proceeded to exceed expectations.

JEFF FRANCOEUR CELEBRATES A HOME RUN WITH HIS NEW TEAMMATES IN NEW YORK DURING A 2009 GAME. FRANCOEUR'S UPPER-BODY STRENGTH IS GENERATED THROUGH AN INTENSE WORKOUT PROGRAM.

In the following pages, Francoeur discusses his difficult decision to give up football and how he handled the enormous demands to succeed in his own backyard. After appearing in the April 2007 issue of *STACK* Magazine, Francoeur highlighted his second professional season with 29 HRs and 103 RBIs. He was clearly considered one of the game's bright young stars. Unfortunately, his aura was tarnished in 2008, when the Braves unceremoniously sent the future cornerstone of their franchise back to the minors to fine-tune his skills. However, Francoeur is a humble athlete who is driven to excel, so this surprising setback did not alter his quest to be the best. After a 2009 mid-season trade to the Mets, Francoeur left his beloved home for a new challenge. But rest assured: his home never abandoned him.

SAFE AT HOME

Jeff Francoeur has been living the dream. He spent his teen years at Parkview High School in Lilburn, Georgia, starring at wide receiver and safety on the football team and leading the baseball squad to the Georgia 5-A state championship. Although he turned down a full ride to play football at Clemson, Jeff's life read even more like a storybook when his hometown Atlanta Braves drafted him in 2002.

A cannon-armed outfielder, Jeff steadily and successfully climbed the minor-league ladder during his first few seasons, and in 2005, he was called to the Show. Once in the lineup, the young right fielder needed little time to win over the fans at Turner Field with his speed, powerful swing, and strong arm. During his rookie campaign, he was third in the league in outfield assists while swatting 14 homers and 35 extra base hits—despite playing only half the season. This amazing tear put Jeff in the spotlight and created expectations for big numbers. Although he now has a few good seasons under his belt and is known as one of the top young players in baseball, Jeff, who lives just a few miles from where he grew up, remains grounded in his faith and his desire to improve by working hard on his body and game.

Recently, we met up with Jeff during one of his frequent returns to Parkview, where he chatted with current Panther players and old coaches, grabbed a workout, and reminisced about his high school days.

Will somebody please pinch this guy?

STACK: What's it like playing in the big leagues for your hometown team?

JF: It's awesome. Think about it. I drive down to the stadium, which is only 25 minutes from where I grew up. All my friends and family can come to every game, and the whole town watches us, because everyone here loves the Braves.

STACK: We're sitting at your high school, with your elementary school right behind us. How do you feel being back here?

JF: Oh man, all the memories come back. I remember everything from elementary school—from field day to the 60-yard dash. The coolest thing is looking back over those 13 years and seeing how I matured into a man and an athlete over that time. Looking at myself from kindergarten all the way up until my senior year in high school makes me realize how much I learned each day and how much I grew up. It's great being able to come around here and look at where I came from.

STACK: Do you have any particularly fond athletic memories from your high school career?

JF: The biggest one occurred on the football field over there. It was an interception return I had my senior year against our big rival, Brookwood, which is about six miles down the road on Five Forks. We were up 14–7 with about a minute left in the third quarter. They had just driven 80 yards on us and were on our 16-yard line. Their quarterback tried to throw an out pass. I picked it off and took it back 86 yards for a touchdown. I was running right down our sideline, so all I saw was a sea of orange as our fans stood up and went crazy. It was the coolest seven or eight seconds of running I've ever done.

STACK: Who were, or still are, your biggest influences around here?

JF: My coaches—Coach Buchanan for

baseball and Coaches Flowe and Whitley for football. Then there are other guys, like Larry and Roy Massey. They treat me like the same old Jeff when I come back here; that's what's great about returning to see them. I know that I can always come here to get away, grab a workout, have some privacy and relax. That's the fun part—just hanging out with some hometown people who are excited to see me.

STACK: Turning down an offer to play football or baseball in college to go straight to the pros—was that a hard decision to make?

JF: Yes, especially when I was eighteen and all my friends were going to college. You look forward to that experience of having Saturday games and enjoying some basketball games in the off-season. At the same time, though, I realized that I had to sacrifice good times in college and be on road trips, sometimes for 12 hours, to get where I wanted to go. Trust me, it is all worth it when you make it to the big stage.

STACK: How well did you adjust to major league ball?

JF: I think it went well because of the solid background I had in strength and lifting, which I got here. We had a really established weight system at Parkview, so I didn't have much trouble switching from aluminum to wooden bats, which poses a problem for most guys.

STACK: How did the hype and high expectations after your amazing rookie season affect your development as a player?

JF: It was tough to deal with right away, but Bobby [Cox] did a great job of bringing me along. I'll never forget the first three weeks; he only played me against left-handed pitchers. We had a four-game series in San Francisco. I sat out the first three games, then pinch-hit in the fourth. It was tough because I had never done that; I was used to playing all the time. Then he

gave me a chance to play against Washington, and they were pitching a righty. I had two home runs, so he started putting me in the lineup every day. He helped me build confidence, then let me go from there.

STACK: How did it feel to belt a three-run homer as your first big-league hit?

JF: That was awesome. What people don't realize is that until that point I was 0–3 with 2 Ks. I had a 3–2 count against Glendon Rush in the eighth inning, and it was just awesome. The ball might have been a few feet off the ground; it was just a line drive to center. I was saying "Get up!" and just kept running.

STACK: You put on 15 pounds of muscle before the 2006 season. What inspired you to do that?

JF: One thing I've always tried to keep is my work ethic. I never want to be outworked. I didn't want to settle for one good game or even a good season. I've always said, "Don't try to be good; be great," and then, "Don't just be great; be the best." When you keep striving to be the best, you'll come into your own. I think people get lackadaisical, focusing on what they did last season, then resting on their good power numbers. The truth is, though, you can always do better. The day I lose that work ethic will be the day I'll know it's time to get out of the game.

STACK: Have you always understood the importance of preparation?

JF: Yes. Preparation, discipline, and perseverance—getting after it every day—are the most important things in athletics.

STACK: What are some of your goals this year regarding your training and your body?

JF: One thing I wasn't happy with last year was that although I'm a pretty fast guy, I stole only one base. I am really working on that. I want to get back to being more of an athlete,

so I've gone back to my football work, and started training with Chip Smith. I'm hoping that will pay off for me. Chip has an amazing track record with the NFL Combine guys who come through his facility. I'm working to get that mentality back.

STACK: Ever had to prove your ability to doubters?

JF: Absolutely. Some people overrate you; some underrate you. But it's important to keep your mind on those who underrate you, so you can go out there and prove what you can do. With my game, critics always talk about me being aggressive or free swinging at the plate, but that's who I am and how I play. So I just go out and play the best I can.

STACK: Can you explain why Joshua 1:19 is written on your batting gloves?

JF: My mom read that verse to me over and over when I was in the hospital after surgery. To me, it means that I can go into any situation—in sports or life—and the Lord has commanded me to be strong and not afraid. As a Christian, I have nothing to be afraid of on the field. At the end of the day, all that really matters to me is that Christ died for my sins. When you know that, it makes going out there and playing a lot easier. You have nothing to worry about, because He will take care of you.

STACK: What kind of player do you want to be next season? A few years from now?

JF: I have always wanted to be the best, and that is what I strive for. But more than that, I want people to say, "That guy played hard. He put it on the line and played with great character and integrity." To me, the best way to be remembered is as an awesome teammate by the guys who played with you.

STACK: Do you have any specific goals for the season?

JF: I set some personal goals before last season, but making the playoffs this year is even more important. I want to get back that taste of the playoffs I once had. Playing Houston was so much fun. The whole atmosphere was great, so to feel that again would make me very happy. Playing in October is fun—not watching it from home.

STACK: Are you comfortable in the spotlight and being looked at as a role model?

JF: Absolutely, I am very comfortable. You have to humble yourself and realize that the good Lord puts you in certain situations for a reason. All of us athletes—whether we like it or not—have to be role models for kids, and I get really frustrated with guys who don't think they have to. I just want to tell them that being a good role model is part of their job. I enjoy kids and signing for them, because they are the future of the game. It means so much more to them then it does to some adult.

STACK: What is your inspiration when baseball—or life in general—isn't going your way?

JF: When things aren't going great, keep going and fight through.... James 1:2 talks about it, and I love it. To me, life is about persevering. It won't always be great, and you'll have your ups and downs. Some weeks in baseball, you'll get 12 hits, and other weeks you'll only get one. Just persevere and be your best.

STACK: What would you say to a high school athlete who is just starting his playing career?

JF: Just enjoy the experience. Play as many sports as possible, and enjoy hanging out with your friends. Just be a kid, and have fun in whatever sport you play.

EXERCISES

1 PULL-UPS

- Grab pull-up bar with overhand, shoulder-width grip

- Pull body up until chin is above bar

- Lower with control until arms are straight; repeat movement

Benefits: Strengthens back, shoulders, scapular region, and arms for improved bat speed and power

COACHING POINTS

➡ **Avoid rocking or kicking legs for momentum**
➡ **Focus on full range of motion**

2 DIPS

- Grasp handles of dip machine and support body with straight arms

- Lower with control until chest is at hand level

- Push up until arms are straight; repeat movement

Benefits: Stronger chest, shoulders, and triceps for added power at the plate

COACHING POINTS

➡ **Maintain erect upper-body posture**
➡ **Avoid rocking or kicking legs for momentum**

SHOULDER FRONT RAISE

- Hold light dumbbell or plate in each hand in front of thighs

- Raise dumbbells in front of body until hands reach upper-chest level

- Lower dumbbells slowly to start position; repeat movement

Benefits: Increased shoulder stability for arm strength and injury prevention

COACHING POINTS

- ➥ Avoid raising dumbbells too high
- ➥ Use slow movements

SHOULDER SIDE RAISE

- Hold light dumbbell or plate in each hand with arms at sides

- Raise dumbbells to shoulder level with palms facing floor

- Lower dumbbells slowly to start position; repeat movement

Benefits: Increased shoulder stability for arm strength and injury prevention

COACHING POINTS

- ➥ Avoid raising dumbbells too high
- ➥ Use slow movements
- ➥ Do not create discomfort in shoulders

EMPTY CAN

- Hold light dumbbell or plate in each hand with arms at sides

- Raise dumbbells to shoulder level, with thumbs to floor and pinkies to ceiling

- Lower dumbbells slowly to start position; repeat movement

Benefits: Increased shoulder stability for arm strength and injury prevention

Coaching Points

- Avoid raising dumbbells too high
- Use slow, controlled movements
- Do not create discomfort in shoulders

6 PARTNER MED BALL ROTATION

- Holding med ball in front of you, stand back-to-back with partner

- Rotate right; hand med ball to partner

- Rotate left, receive med ball from partner; repeat continuously

COACHING POINTS

- ➡ Start with light med ball; progress to heavier weight after perfecting technique
- ➡ Do not rush through movement
- ➡ Avoid rocking or swaying legs to create momentum
- ➡ Isolate and focus on core rotation and movement

Benefits: Improved rotational core strength and flexibility for batting power and injury prevention

7 FOREARM CURLS

- Sit on bench holding barbell or dumbbells so that forearms rest on thighs

- Using only wrists and without moving arms, curl weight toward chest

- Lower weight with control as far as wrists allow; repeat

Benefits: Strengthened grip for better bat control and power

COACHING POINTS

- ➡ Start with light weight; progress to heavier weight after perfecting technique
- ➡ Focus on full range of motion for wrists

UPPER BODY WORKOUT

EXERCISE	SETS/REPS
Pull-Ups	2x as many as possible
Dips	2x as many as possible
Shoulder Front Raise	2x10
Shoulder Side Raise	2x10
Empty Can	2x10
Partner Med Ball Rotation	2x10 each direction
Forearm Curls	2x20

CHAPTER 6

JUSTIN VERLANDER

EDITOR'S NOTE

Generally speaking, pitchers and quarterbacks are reputed to be pretty-boy prima donnas who operate on their own schedules. As Justin Verlander rolled up to the Detroit Tigers' training facility in Lakeland, Florida, in his shiny new Porsche, he seemed to fit the stereotype. From the moment he stepped out of the car, however, Verlander behaved in a manner that shattered it—and then some.

The Detroit Tigers ace did operate on his own schedule, but in a good way, since he spent most of the winter in Lakeland. Verlander showed up several weeks before his major league teammates. Together with a smattering of minor league prospects, he performed daily workouts to strengthen his legs and upper body for the season ahead—all with the help of Tigers strength and conditioning coach Javair Gillett.

Our prior work with Gillett had revealed the efficacy of his training; so when the coach suggested a cover feature with Justin, based on his performance on the mound and hard work in the weight room, we were glad to oblige.

JUSTIN VERLANDER DELIVERS A PITCH DURING A 2007 SPRING TRAINING GAME. VERLANDER'S WORKOUTS FOCUS ON THE FULL-BODY ACTIVITY HE USES IN MAJOR LEAGUE GAMES.

Following our interview and video shoot with Verlander, his performance throughout the 2008 season fell short of his usual standard. His ERA ballooned to 4.84, and his win-loss record fell to a disappointing 11–17, down from 18–6 the previous season. But through it all, the big right-hander [6'5", 225-pound] refused to stop battling. Many speculated that Verlander wasn't at full health throughout the season, an assumption that gained support when he returned to form in 2009, tearing through the early months of the season. Naturally, non-prima-donna Verlander credited his renewed success to another off-season in Lakeland with Gillett.

This is the Justin Verlander cover feature as it originally appeared in the May/June 2008 issue of *STACK* Magazine.

RADAR GAMES

The chorus of Notorious B.I.G.'s "Victory" kicks in as Justin Verlander steps under a bar loaded with 365 pounds for the second time in the past few minutes. While Verlander is pounding out one of his final sets of squats, there are few other Major Leaguers to be found at the Tigers' spring training facility in Lakeland, Florida. It's the middle of winter, and Justin has been at this for weeks. It's just him, Biggie, and the expert tutelage of strength and conditioning coach Javair Gillett. This isn't what you'd expect from a well-paid major-league pitcher with two successful years behind him. But this is how Justin spent his winter break.

Justin Verlander once hurled a baseball at 102 miles per hour. In the ninth inning of his no-hitter against the Brewers in June 2007, Verlander was clocked at 101 mph. Those frightening three-digit numbers are what make Verlander one of the best pitchers in the majors and the ace of the Detroit Tigers. "It's all about the fastball," Verlander says with a grin. "That's my way of challenging guys. That's the best, when you just blow one by a guy. I live for that one-on-one competition out there. On the mound, it's me versus you, and that's what I love about it. When a good hitter comes up, it's like, 'Here we go.'"

That this confidence is completely absent of cockiness is in a large part due to the guidance Verlander received from his parents early on. Verlander recalls, "When I first started pitching, I had a really good game, and in the car on the way home I said, 'Man, I am good!' Immediately my parents turned around. They told me it was OK to think I was good, but don't go saying those things. There's a difference between confidence and cockiness. Stay on the side of confidence and don't be a jerk."

Although this was a great piece of advice, it wasn't long before Verlander taught his old man a lesson of his own. While out in the country in Virginia, Verlander and his father stumbled upon a lake with a dirt road alongside it—the perfect setting for father and son to share a moment tossing rocks into the lake. "But before

I knew it, we were getting into a little throwing contest," Verlander says. "He was throwing them about halfway across the lake, and I was clearing the whole thing. I looked over at him, and he was already looking at me. Here's this grown man, and I'm a 10-year old out-throwing him!"

The same freakish power that left his father fuming made Verlander every little league parent's worst nightmare. "Back then, I never knew where the ball was going," he says, "I always had a really good arm, but I used to make kids on deck cry because I'd hit so many batters. It's pretty funny now when I look back on it, but back then parents didn't like me and didn't want me to be allowed to pitch." Some kids ended up quitting, while others refused to step into the box against Verlander.

Verlander eventually developed control during his awkward teenage years—he was 6'2", 150 pounds, with size 14 feet at the age of 14. His parents described him as "a Brontosaurus clobbering down the basepaths with flippers on." As he matured, he became dangerous on the mound for reasons other than plunking opposing batters. Over the span of his high school career, Verlander grew into his body and became the best pitcher in the Richmond, Virginia, area. That wasn't enough for Major League Baseball scouts and even big-time college coaches to take a chance.

Old Dominion was pretty much the only school that came knocking, and Verlander obliged, "There was no recruiting process for me," he says. "Old Dominion was the only school interested in me early on, so I committed." Verlander soon thereafter rewrote the Monarchs' record books. He posted a 1.90 ERA his freshman season as the number-one hurler, and went on to strike out 17 batters in a game against James Madison. By 2004,

Verlander had exploded into a feared 6'5", 200-pound menace on the mound—too much for pro scouts to pass up a second time. He was selected by the Tigers with the second overall pick in the 2004 MLB Draft.

After two successful seasons, Verlander put it all together in 2007. He fanned 183 batters while going 18-6 for the Tigers.

Verlander's improvements on the mound have directly coincided with his devotion to training. "I didn't get into training until kind of late," Verlander says. "When I got to college, I first started working out and saw some gains in my on-field performance. I went into college weighing 170, and during my first semester I put on 25 pounds. My upper body stayed the same, but my legs got a lot stronger. I went from 93 miles per hour to 97 in the course of year. But it still really didn't sink in, I [worked out] because I had to."

When Verlander got to the majors and saw how the long season could cause his body to break down, he then realized what it took to stay afloat. "I couldn't sustain myself for

162 games without the physical preparation in the off-season," he says. "That was three years ago when I realized it, so this is my second off-season of really working hard and getting into [a training program]. Last year, I saw big improvements because of it."

During those three years, Tigers strength and conditioning coach Javair Gillett has been creating workouts to turn Verlander's body into a resilient, powerful fastball machine. "He's really good at individualizing workouts," Verlander says. "I came in [and] told him that I wanted to get stronger here and gain some weight, and he individualized the workout for me. It's nice that he's researching and doing his homework on new techniques out there."

Gillett's program seeks to get Verlander's lower body as strong as possible over the off-season and then build his explosiveness and

power as spring season approaches. "He's been gifted with natural athleticism," Gillett says. "He's a very powerful athlete naturally, so he's not just starting to learn how to balance and coordinate his body. He already has that, so now it's just about maximizing it. He came in as a young athlete, just learning what to do on a daily basis going from college to the professional level. As a starter, he has time between his starts, which is preparation time that he needs to spend improving his performance and all aspects."

Much of what Gillett has created for Verlander involves having the star pitcher work on controlling his body in an effort to increase his performance in less-than-ideal positions. "We start with a lot of balance and agility movements," Gillett says. "Then we work our way into baseball-specific stuff that prepares him to react in different directions after he throws the ball. We are getting him ready to perform in awkward positions, like when he's going down to field a baseball and has to pop up very quickly."

Besides wanting to have the biggest legs on the team (he had a couple players to pass heading into spring training), Verlander hasn't set any goals for himself this year. "Let's say I want to be a 20-game winner," he says. "What if I win 20 games and have three starts left? It would be very easy for me to say, I'm right where I wanted to be, so I don't have to do anything more. I don't set baseball goals, because I know that if I take it one game at a time and do everything I can for that one game, that's a good approach for me."

We observed Verlander going through his brutal "power day" with Gillett last winter. The intensity was high throughout as Verlander tore through his balance, agility, speed, explosiveness, and lower-body strengthening exercises. This is where velocity is born.

FIELD WORK

1 HIP POPPERS

Gillett: "These work on the baseball-specific movements that he's doing on the mound—pickoffs or just getting off the mound quickly. Start the movement with the hips—hop, rotate the feet, land, and pop back. We'll go up to 180- and even 360-degree hops."

Verlander: "This touches on the hips, speed, and quickness—all things I want to work on so that I can field at my position a little better. This helps getting off the mound, getting to ground balls or bunts or covering first."

- Stand with left foot in speed ladder and right foot outside

- Quickly pop hips and rotate left to land facing opposite direction with right foot in ladder and left foot out

- Immediately pop hips and rotate right to return to start position

- Repeat continuously for specified duration

2 HALF MOON STEPPING WITH FOOTBALL

Gillett: "This helps improve the efficiency of his first step. In baseball, a lot of movement is from a stationary position. After throwing a pitch, he waits, then has to react. Whether he steps with his right or left foot, at some point he has to slow down. This teaches acceleration and deceleration."

- Place five cones in semi-circle and one additional cone at center

- Stand at center cone with semi-circle to left and partner outside semi-circle

- As partner tosses football to each cone in semi-circle, step toward cone with left leg and catch ball

- Toss ball back and step back to center cone

- Repeat continuously for all five cones

- Perform to opposite side, stepping with right leg

Gillett: "This works on getting into the right position—low with a wide base. Start slowing down with the back leg first and then get on that front leg. If your weight is too far on that front leg, you're going to keep going forward. I incorporate a baseball because it makes him more efficient, since fielding a ball comes so naturally to him. He's been doing this for a while, so the stamina and conditioning are there, and I can shorten the recovery."

Verlander: "Just like everything we do outside, it's got some conditioning to it. It's also a mental thing for me. You have to focus because you have to get your footwork right, but you also have to think about catching the ball."

- Place five cones in semi-circle with additional cone at center

- Stand at center cone with semi-circle to left and partner outside of semi-circle

- As partner rolls baseball to each cone in semi-circle, sprint to cone, break down, and field ball

- Toss ball back and backpedal to center cone

- Repeat continuously for all five cones

- Perform set with semi-circle to right

4 OVERHEAD MED BALL THROWS

Gillett: "This is a modification of Olympic lifts. It's lighter weight, so you can move it very quickly. Throw it straight up, and the ball will naturally go behind you. Get your hips, knees and ankles all extending when you drive through the ground."

Verlander: "I like these because you have to incorporate your whole body into it, especially legs and core and a little upper body. For me, legs and core are the two biggest things."

- Assume athletic stance, holding med ball in front

- Lower into squat and explode through hips, knees, and ankles to throw med ball as high as possible

- Run to med ball, pick it up; repeat

5 BACKHAND/FOREHAND MED BALL TOSS

Gillett: "This is a plyometric, multiple-response exercise. We are training the legs to explode powerfully, and the med ball works core stability, balance, reaction and hand-eye coordination. He's working on trying to get as high as possible. He's really got to stick that landing, because he's got to get down and drive himself back up again. When he has to go down and grab the ball and throw off balance to first, it will be a little easier for him to control his body."

Verlander: "This was one of the first times I've done this. It takes a ton of coordination."

- With partner to right, assume split-squat stance with left leg forward

- When partner tosses ball to you, catch it, jump vertically, rotate hips right, and throw ball back

- Land facing opposite direction in split-squat position with right leg forward

- Repeat back and forth in continuous fashion for specified reps

STRENGTH WORK

1 SIX-PACK SCAP ROUTINE

Gillett: "To me, the core spans all along your spine through your hips, including the scap muscles. It's a good exercise, where you might not even need resistance until you progress. Pinch your scaps together and keep your shoulders down. Everyone talks about the rotator cuff, which consists of four muscles that stabilize the shoulder girdle, but they forget about the scaps, which is your shoulder blade area. If they do not move properly, it's going to cause instability in that shoulder."

Verlander: "I do it before my workout and then do manual resistance strengthening at the end. Right now, I'm strengthening, then during the season, I maintain."

- Position physioball on incline bench and attach surgical tubing underneath bench

- Lie with stomach on ball, holding tubing in each hand

- Brings arms to each position below; hold for six seconds

- Repeat for specified reps

   Arms in front in V, thumbs up
   Arms in front in V, palms down
   Arms to side, thumbs up
   Arms to side, palms down
   Elbows at 90, shoulders at 90, thumbs up
   Elbows at 90, shoulders at 90, palms down

2 SPLIT-SQUAT ON 2X4

Gillett: "In most lunges, people have their feet at shoulder-width, but when you're standing on the board, they're in a straight line. As far as baseball players, you're in a straight line when you are coming to field a ground ball on the forehand or backhand side. Sometimes you even cross over your body. You need to make sure that your hips stay straight and go straight up and straight down. Don't lean to one side."

- Holding dumbbell in one hand, assume split-squat stance on 2x4 with opposite leg forward

- Lower into split squat, bringing dumbbell toward front foot

- Drive up into start position; repeat for specified reps

- Perform set with other leg forward and dumbbell in opposite hand

3 SQUAT

Gillett: "This hits every lower body muscle and is a great lower back and abdominal strength exercise. If you want to have power and the ability to push off and deliver a ball at a high velocity, you have to strengthen your lower body and have a strong core group of muscles. Justin has been able to do this exercise with me and in college, so he's pretty good at it and believes in it. The drop set at the end is all about having the stamina to perform in the ninth inning."

Verlander: "Although I'm really careful with my upper body, I like being able to get my legs stronger by really blowing them out in the weight room."

- Assume athletic position with bar on back and feet slightly wider than hip width

- Keeping chest up, core tight, and knees behind toes, lower into squat until tops of thighs are parallel to ground

- Drive up, out of squat position

- Repeat for specified reps

Note: Immediately after last set, lighten weight and perform 10 reps

4 DUMBBELL WALKING LUNGE

Gillett: "This is more of a one-legged stability exercise that works a little more glute and hip strength. We really want to make sure that the glutes and hamstrings are strong heading into the season. The glutes are where a pitcher generates his power. If they're not strong, it puts the hamstrings at risk of injury."

- Assume athletic stance holding dumbbells at side [or wearing weighted vest]

- Step forward with right leg and lower into lunge position with front knee behind toes

- Drive up and step forward with left leg and lower into lunge position

- Repeat continuously for specified reps

5 SINGLE-LEG SQUAT

Gillett: "I want him to be able to decelerate and explode on one leg, and that one leg has to be strong so that it can support the body weight. When you're moving at a high rate and you have to stop on a dime, the natural force of gravity and momentum put a lot of load on your leg."

- Stand on one leg on top of box

- Keeping knee behind toes, lower into squat until top of thigh is almost parallel to ground

- Drive up into start position; repeat for specified reps

- Perform set with other leg

6 HAMSTRING CURLS ON BALL

Gillett: "This is a two-joint movement as opposed to the single-joint movement of lying on a machine and doing a leg curl. Your hip and knee joints need to be put though a range of motion. We move into this as we get close to the season and then into the season. It's working stability a little more. You have to get the glutes to fire before the hamstrings."

- Lie on back with heels on top of physioball

- Raise hips so that body forms straight line from feet to shoulders

- Keeping hips elevated, curl heels toward butt to roll physioball toward you

- Slowly straighten legs to roll ball away from you

- Repeat for specified reps

Note: Partner can apply resistance to ball to increase difficulty

PHYSIOBALL REVERSE GLUTE/HYPEREXTENSION

Gillett: "It's important to get the glutes and lower back strong. Strong glutes take pressure off the back. It's not about working the lower back; it's about squeezing the butt and getting the range of motion until you're in a straight line. Don't hyperextend to where your feet go over your body. Get to straight and relax your hamstrings as much as possible."

- Position physioball on incline bench and lie with stomach on ball

- Keeping legs straight, raise them until body forms straight line

- Lower with control and repeat for specified reps

FLAMINGOS/SINGLE-LEG STRAIGHT-LEG DEADLIFT COMBO

Gillett: "At first, he's not moving. He just has to stop the ball, stabilize and try not to lose balance. Then [he has to get] back up and throw it a little further—so he's got to reach for it and do a one-legged, stiff-legged deadlift. When he comes out to catch, he's really got to slow the ball down, then bring it down to his toes. He comes back up and actually tosses it with his lower back and glutes in a powerful manner."

Verlander: "You wouldn't think this is working you very much, but when he's throwing the ball and you're stabilizing on the pad, you're using your core more than you think."

- Stand on one leg with foot on stability pad

- As partner tosses med ball, catch it, stabilize body, and toss ball back

- After specified reps, partner will then toss ball low and in front of you

- Catch ball in front and continue to lower upper body into Single-Leg, Straight-Leg Deadlift

- Return to standing position and toss ball back to partner

- Repeat for specified sets

- Perform combination set on other leg

JUSTIN VERLANDER'S TRAINING GUIDE

FIELD WORK	WEEK 1	WEEK 2	WEEK 3
Hip Poppers	3 sets/ 45-second rest	3 sets/ 45-second rest	3 sets/ 45-second rest
Half Moon Stepping With Football	3 sets each side/ 45-second rest	3 sets each side/ 45-second rest	3 sets each side/ 30–45-second rest
Half Moon Fielding With Baseball	3 sets each side/ 45-second rest	3 sets each side/ 45-second rest	3 sets each side/ 30–45-second rest
Overhead Med Ball Throws	3x10	3x10	3x10
Backhand/Forehand Med Ball Toss	3x10 each side/ 45-second rest	3x10 each side/ 45-second rest	3x10 each side/ 30–45-second rest

STRENGTH WORK	WEEK 1	WEEK 2	WEEK 3
Split-Squat on 2x4	2x10	2x10	2x8
Squat	4x10	2x10, 3x8	2x10, 3x8
DB Walking Lunge	3x10 each leg	3x10 each leg	3x8 each leg
Single-Leg Squat	none	none	3x6
Hamstring Curls on Ball	3x10	3x10	3x10
Physioball Reverse Glute/Hyperextension	3x10	3x10	3x10
Barbell or DB Straight-Leg Deadlift	3x10	3x10	none
Flamingos and Single-Leg Straight-Leg Deadlift Combo	none	none	1x15+8
Six-Pack Scap Routine	6x6 seconds	6x6 seconds	6x6 seconds

FIELD WORK	WEEK 4	WEEK 5	WEEK 6
Hip Poppers	3 sets/ 45-second rest	3 sets/ 45-second rest	3 sets/ 45-second rest
Half Moon Stepping With Football	3 sets each side/ 20–30-second rest	3 sets each side/ 10–20-second rest	3 sets each side/ 10-second rest
Half Moon Fielding With Baseball	3 sets each side/ 20–30-second rest	3 sets each side/ 10–20-second rest	3 sets each side/ 10-second rest
Overhead Med Ball Throws	3x10 inside cage	3x10 inside cage	3x10 inside cage
Backhand/Forehand Med Ball Toss	3x10 each side/ 20–30-second rest	3x10 each side/ 10–20-second rest	3x10 each side/ 10-second rest

STRENGTH WORK	WEEK 4	WEEK 5	WEEK 6
Split-Squat on 2x4	2x8	2x6	2x6
Squat	1x10, 2x8, 2x6	1x10, 1x8, 3x6	1x10, 4x6
DB Walking Lunge	3x8 each leg	3x6 each leg	3x6 each leg with heavier weight
Single-Leg Squat	3x6	3x8	3x10
Hamstring Curls on Ball	3x10 add partner resistance	3x10 add partner resistance	3x10 add partner resistance
Physioball Reverse Glute/Hyperextension	3x10	3x10	3x10
Barbell or DB Straight-Leg Deadlift	none	none	none
Flamingos and Single-Leg Straight-Leg Deadlift Combo	2x15+8	2x15+8	3x15+8
Six-Pack Scap Routine	6x6 seconds	6x6 seconds	6x6 seconds

CHAPTER 7

JIMMY ROLLINS

EDITOR'S NOTE

Without a doubt, Jimmy Rollins is the most enthusiastic cover athlete we've ever worked with. Our original plan was to spend a day with Rollins to document one of his off-season strength and speed workouts. But the Phillies star shortstop loved the idea so much that he invited us to stick around to watch his batting drills the following day. In most cases, professional athletes are understandably stingy with their time, so this offer was somewhat surprising.

Even more surprising was the fact that Rollins made his training home at Springside, a private, all-girls school on the outskirts of Philadelphia, where Rollins knew many of the faculty and students by name, and no one seemed particularly impressed that the 2007 National League MVP hit up their weight room every day.

A defining moment with Rollins came toward the end of our interview. A STACK staffer had a 12-year-old nephew, a huge Major League Baseball fan, who was stricken with cancer and heading into his first chemo treatment. The staffer asked Rollins if he would tape a quick video message to his nephew. Rollins did that—and so much more. He created the message, signed the

SPEED IS A MAJOR PART OF JIMMY ROLLINS' GAME. SHOWN HERE RUNNING THE BASES IN A 2009 GAME, ROLLINS WORKS ON HIS SPEED THROUGHOUT THE OFFSEASON.

hat he was wearing for the boy and dedicated his first home run of the season to the youngster. At a later date, Rollins made arrangements with the child's father for the boy to spend some time with him on the field before a game.

His kindness and compassion make Rollins forever one of our favorites. When he went on to lead the Phillies to the 2008 World Series title, we couldn't have been happier for him and his team.

This is the Jimmy Rollins cover feature as it first appeared in the March 2008 issue of *STACK* Magazine.

THE TALENTED MR. ROLLINS

Fresh off scoring the Minor League Player of the Year award, an 18-year-old baseball player is handed an official scouting report from his own organization, the Philadelphia Phillies. The words on the page seem to make no sense to the kid, who's been dreaming of playing Major League baseball since he was eight years old, who worked to get *five* swings by shagging *hundreds* of balls during his mother's softball practices, and who watched Rickey Henderson religiously to learn the art of base theft.

One line in the report stuck out, and he kept reading it over and over: "Jimmy Rollins has reached his peak in this game. He will not play at the next level."

While some players, after being judged this way, would've called it a day and hung up their cleats, the young J-Roll used it as his motivation to take over the game of baseball. In fact, the explosive shortstop was far from done. "I was 18 years old; I had a lot of baseball left in me," Rollins says. "I had a lot of growing up and learning to do, [so] I wasn't mad at them for

making those reports, but it forced me to look at myself and step up."

Rollins' new source of motivation coincided with a changing of the guard in Philly, setting up a historic course. "Fortunately, we brought in a whole new regime and started from scratch," Rollins recalls. "Lee Elliott, a really good man, brought me into his office and read me those reports. He tore them up and threw them in the garbage can right in front of me. He told me to prove those reports wrong. Two years later, I was in the big leagues."

Rollins did more than just make it to the Show. Since 1997, when that report was handed down, Rollins has racked up a handful of All-Star appearances as one of the best defensive shortstops and all-around hitters in the game. His most impressive feat, however, came in 2007 in the form of a National League MVP. "I don't really know what criteria it takes to be an MVP in any sport," Rollins says. "When I started hearing my name mentioned, I was like, 'Are these dudes for real?' I asked myself, 'What am I doing that's so special?' I felt like I had so

much more I could do. I could be a better hitter, a better runner, and a better fielder."

During his MVP campaign, J-Roll made history as the fourth player ever to hit 20 home runs, 20 triples, 20 doubles, and steal 20 bases in the same season. Throw in his .296 batting average and you have an obscene amount of offensive output from the diminutive game-breaker. The all-around nature of Rollins' game indicates a special ability that goes beyond the physical; he has an intricate knowledge of the game, which he got from his mother. "She was a thinker when she played softball," Rollins says. "She was thinking two to three plays ahead, so when the situation arose, she knew how to react. My game strategy came from her."

Polishing those mom-instilled strategizing skills and taking them to another level was his father's doing. "We used to go to Oakland A's games," Rollins says. "I was just there to watch my favorite players and smell the sweet tobacco. Then one day, my father says to me, 'Tell me what's going on in the game.' I told him I just wanted to watch. He told me, 'No, you study the game.' It took me three or four times watching to figure out what he wanted me to do, [but] then I understood what baseball was—why he didn't pitch to the guy or why he hit the cut-off man, while I'm up there screaming for him to throw out the runner at home."

Rollins combines his knowledge of the game with athleticism and surprising power to create a near perfect package. He is always stumped when he's asked how someone his size—5'8", 175 pounds—hits 30 home runs. "I don't know how I have power, but I've always surprised people," he says. "I guess it just comes from when I was younger and my father used to say, 'Be strong.' I just look for what I can do to the best of my abilities. For example, I know

this: I'm going to be short, I'm going to be fast, and I'm going to be strong. I'm never going to hit the ball as far or as majestic as Ryan Howard or Barry Bonds. But if the wall is 330 feet away, and I hit it 332 feet, I get the same result. If the bases are loaded, it's a grand slam."

His shots might lack the wow factor of a Ryan Howard slam, but Rollins has always satisfied the fans with his upbeat attitude and Bay Area swagger, two quickly evolving J-Roll trademarks. "Some athletes forget how blessed we are to be able to do this," he says with a smile. "We have great health, and we are doing something we love. When I'm in a rut, I take a step back onto the grass and look into the stands and see all the people who came to watch us play baseball. I was once that kid in the stands wanting to play. They want to see me run, see me hit, and see me entertain. They didn't pay money to see me be a robot and head directly to the dugout. I signed up for this. Nobody made me play baseball."

The Philly faithful were definitely entertained in 2007 during the Phillies' epic end-of-the-season playoff clinch and Rollins' 20–20–20–20 MVP explosion, which he topped off with a triple in his last at bat of the season—in true J-Roll style. And while he knows that Philly fans and baseball pundits tend to overhype awards and place undue pressure on repeating, Rollins doesn't care. "No one can put more pressure or expect more out of me than myself," he says. "I want to go out there and gain the respect of my peers. I want them to know I was great defensively, I was a pain on the base paths and I could hit with power. I go out to be the best. The awards can come later."

With the NL MVP still sinking in and the new season upon him, Rollins must look forward and find a way to improve on history. Maybe he should turn to what he calls the best piece of advice he ever received. "It was 1996—my senior year in high school—when the Seattle Mariners were thinking about taking me in the second round," he says. "I went up to Seattle and got to meet Ken Griffey Jr. Grif pulled me aside and told me, 'Whatever you're doing, keep doing it. They're drafting you for a reason. Along the way, you're going to have a lot of guys trying to change you, tell you what to do and what your best assets are. But at the end of the day, you're the one who has to answer the bell.'"

Keep doing what you're doing, Jimmy.

Control Your Body, Control the Game

Twice a week throughout this off-season, Rollins hands himself over to Aaron Sistrunk, strength and conditioning coach at Chestnut Hill Academy in Philadelphia. In an effort to make the '07 NL MVP even more valuable, the two men meet at CHA's sister school, Springside, which has amazing fieldhouse facilities.

"With any athlete, I [look for] flaws and figure out how I can make them better," Sistrunk says, "When I first saw Jimmy, I knew I could get him a little bit stronger and a little bit faster to steal more bases. His first three to five steps are amazing, but we've gotten him even faster and a lot stronger. The big thing is his stamina. When we first started, he felt like he was going to throw up. Now he's able to get it done and even crack jokes along the way."

As Rollins tells it, Sistrunk's training keys are core stability, body control, and the ever-painful contrast between the two. "It's all about core and body control," Rollins says. "He loves working contrast so that I'm able to call upon my muscles late in the game. I'm going to need that muscle to steal a bag in the ninth inning to win the game—or in the 14th inning, or when it's real hot in the summer and my body wants to give up."

Sistrunk's contrast method is the reason these training sessions are so grueling. "Contrast means giving him resistance, then taking it away and making him do the same exercise so he can go faster," Sistrunk says. "It's not just a physical thing; it's also a mental thing."

Basically, Sistrunk kicks Rollins' butt, then makes him run when his legs are on fire.

Rollins knew that to build on his impressive performance in 2007, he needed to take his fitness to an even higher level. "I'm looking to reach that peak where my body is in the best shape it can ever be," he says. "You see guys playing football or basketball or baseball, and you look at them and think, 'Man that dude works out hard,' or 'He is really put together.' I want people to look at me and be like, 'Damn, Jimmy's looking good and must be working out. He must be serious and dedicated to his sport.'"

The price for that sort of respect is evident on this day. After an intense dynamic warm-up and quick partner stretch routine, Rollins is physically and mentally prepared to attack what Sistrunk has planned for him. Already dripping with sweat, he looks at Sistrunk and asks, "You gonna kill me again today?" Sistrunk answers with only a smile and walks back out to the center of the gym floor.

Perfect Swings

Three times a week, Rollins meets up with Phillies hitting coach Milt Thompson at the Hit Doctor in Washington Township, New Jersey. These sessions have transformed Rollins into a lumber-wielding student of the game. "I've known Jimmy since 1998," Thompson says. "Since then, he's really grown as a hitter, and he knows himself. He has learned how to play the game and how to prepare himself to play. He'll come back after an at-bat and I won't even have to say anything. He'll know he was too anxious or [that he] dipped his shoulder. He makes great in-game adjustments, even from pitch to pitch."

In order to improve, Rollins seeks perfection in an imperfect skill. "Hitting is the most flawed thing you'll do in any sport," Rollins says. "If you fail 70 percent of the time, you're considered great. But when I'm in the cage—a controlled environment—I have to be perfect. I might have to hit six line drives to get three hits, because three might get caught."

Through a carefully constructed progression, Thompson gets Rollins focused on the key elements of the perfect swing, then builds him up to full-on perfect cuts.

DYNAMIC WARM-UP & STRETCHING

Perform the following drills down and back (20–30 yards each way) in continuous fashion

Sistrunk: "This gets your heart rate up and gets your body warmed up. You have to look at your muscles as a rubber band. If you stretch it when it's cold, it's going to snap. Warm the body up, get the temperature up and then gradually get your body into dynamic stretching, then static stretching. It gets your body prepared mentally and physically to do dynamic movements."

1 HALF-SPEED RUN

- Jog at 50 to 60 percent of max

2 HIGH KNEES

- Rapidly drive knees up with opposite arm/opposite leg action

3 BUTT KICKS

- Kick heels to butt with opposite arm/opposite leg action

4 A-SKIPS

- Skip continuously with knee up/toe up action

5 WALKING LUNGE WITH TWIST

- Step forward with right foot and lower into lunge position

- Keeping chest up, rotate upper body to right

- Repeat with left leg and rotate upper body left

6 STRAIGHT-LEG MARCH

- In alternating and walking fashion, kick straight legs in front to meet hands at shoulder level

7 WALKING KNEE PULLS

- Stand on left foot and pull right knee to chest. Step forward and perform with left knee

8 TOE UPS

- Place right foot in front and extend right leg

- Keeping back flat, reach toward right foot to stretch right hamstring

- Pause, step forward, repeat on left

9 WALKING HEEL PULLS

- Stand on left foot and pull inside of right heel to groin while rotating at right hip

- Step forward and perform on left heel

10 SHUFFLE WITH LATERAL LUNGE

- Shuffle laterally for two strides, pause and perform lateral lunge to right, then left

- Shuffle for two more strides; repeat

- Perform continuously

PARTNER STRETCH

➡ Have partner take the following stretches to a point of tension and hold for 10–15 seconds

➡ Perform 2–3 reps on each side

Sistrunk: "This is to make sure the hamstrings, quads and groins are loosened up. In any sport that requires a lot of side movement, you want to make sure that the groin is strong and loose."

Rollins: "I think it's best to do static stretching with a partner, because you can only stretch yourself so far. Someone else can give you that extra elasticity."

1 STRADDLE (CENTER, RIGHT, LEFT)

- Sit on butt with legs spread wide while partner pushes on back to stretch you forward, to right foot and then to left foot

2 GLUTE

- Lie on back while partner pushes knee into chest

3 HIP ABDUCTOR

- Lie on back while partner pushes knee to chest and rotates leg so that your foot goes toward opposite shoulder

4 HAMSTRING

- Lie on back, with legs extended forward

- Position left foot over partner's shoulder, keeping leg straight

- Partner slowly pushes leg up to point of tension; hold 8–12 seconds

- After release, push against partner's hand for 4–6 seconds

5 LYING TRUNK TWIST

- Lie on back with knees together and bent 90 degrees

- Partner will rotate knees toward floor in one direction and push on chest in the opposite direction

SPEED, AGILITY, AND POWER

1 SPEED LUNGES

Sistrunk: "If Jimmy can lift 500 pounds, that's great. But I'm more concerned with control of your body on the field, so it doesn't always matter how much you can lift."

Rollins: "These burn! You want to cheat by popping up because it hurts so much. But you know if you pop up, you're only cheating yourself. That's where the focus and the dedication to your sport come in. You have to draw on your body to get these things done."

COACHING POINTS

- ➡ Maintain base of support
- ➡ Don't let lunging knee go past big toe
- ➡ Keep abs tight and body controlled

- Step forward with right leg and lower into lunge position until left knee is just off ground. Pause two counts

- Without changing hip or shoulder level, quickly step forward with left leg and lower into lunge position with right knee just off ground

- Pause for two counts

- Repeat over specified distance

- Immediately turn around and sprint back to start line

2 FALLING STARTS

Sistrunk: "This is another way to get his legs back from the speed lunges and improve his body control. We want to make sure he doesn't elevate once he gets his legs underneath him. We want very efficient movement."

- Stand with feet hip-width apart and arms at sides

- Without bending at waist, lean forward as far as possible without tipping over

- Explode into sprint by stepping forward with right foot

- Perform next rep with left leg first

3 RESISTED STARTS

Sistrunk: "This is all contrast. It's giving resistance, and then taking it away so the athlete builds his hamstrings and glutes and learns to accelerate. Keep your nose over your toes, head above shoulders and back straight. We want a fluid movement with elbows at 90 degrees and hands going from hip pocket to eye socket."

Rollins: "Getting pulled is the fun part; it gets your adrenaline going because you want to beat whatever is pulling you back. Running back is the hard part. I fell probably three times when I first started doing these."

- Assume athletic stance with partner providing band resistance from behind

- Explode into sprint and drive arms and legs with proper start technique for specified distance

- Immediately free self from band, turn around and sprint back to start line

4 RESISTED SHUFFLE

Sistrunk: "One of the weakest areas on a man is his hip region, and this helps [work] that. It improves lateral movement and also teaches him to keep his base of support and center of gravity low. Initiate the movement with your inside hip."

- Assume athletic stance with partner providing band resistance from left

- Shuffle right for specified distance while partner provides steady and continuous resistance

- Alternate direction each rep

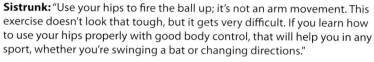

5 OVERHEAD MED BALL THROWS

Sistrunk: "Use your hips to fire the ball up; it's not an arm movement. This exercise doesn't look that tough, but it gets very difficult. If you learn how to use your hips properly with good body control, that will help you in any sport, whether you're swinging a bat or changing directions."

Rollins: "This is my favorite—maybe it's an athlete thing. When you think of power, you just think, 'I want to be strong and show how strong I am.'"

- Holding med ball in front, assume athletic stance

- Lower into squat and explode through hips, knees and ankles to throw med ball as high as possible and slightly back

- Jog to med ball, pick it up, repeat

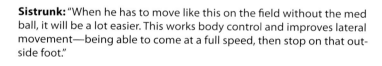

6 GROUND BALLS ON SPEED LADDER WITH MED BALL

Sistrunk: "When he has to move like this on the field without the med ball, it will be a lot easier. This works body control and improves lateral movement—being able to come at a full speed, then stop on that outside foot."

- Holding med ball in front, place left foot in first box of ladder and right foot to outside right

- Lower into ground ball fielding position, gently touching med ball to ground

- Quickly shuffle feet so right foot lands in second box and left foot lands outside and to left

- Immediately lower into ground ball fielding position, gently touching med ball to ground

- Repeat continuously for length of ladder

- Perform backward down length of ladder

STRENGTH

DUMBBELL SQUAT PRESS

Sistrunk: "The 'Arnold' Press works the shoulder girdle and traps. Jimmy has gone up to 50- or 60-pound dumbbells with this."

- Assume stance slightly wider than shoulder width, holding dumbbells at shoulder level, palms facing you

- Lower into squat until top of thighs are parallel to floor

- Drive up out of squat position and press dumbbells overhead while rotating palms away from you

- Return to start position; repeat

COACHING POINTS

- Load hips and fire through
- Keep knees behind big toes
- Keep press motion tight, like you're punching toward ceiling

KETTLEBELL SWINGS

Sistrunk: "Use very light weight with these. It's great for the hips and transverse abdominals, which help with that explosion needed to hit the ball."

- Assume athletic stance with slight knee bend, holding kettlebell in front

- Rotate right and bring kettlebell outside and just below right hip

- Explosively rotate back to center, swinging kettlebell forward and overhead

- Immediately bring kettlebell down and left to outside of left hip

- Repeat back and forth in continuous, controlled fashion

Variation: If kettlebells are not available, perform with 8- to 10-pound med ball

3 INVERTED ROW ON STRAPS

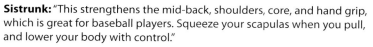

Sistrunk: "This strengthens the mid-back, shoulders, core, and hand grip, which is great for baseball players. Squeeze your scapulas when you pull, and lower your body with control."

Rollins: "If you don't have strong hands, you can't hit a baseball with any power. You'll get the bat knocked out of your hands, as they say."

• Hold handles at end of straps attached to pull-up bar

• Lean back until arms are straight and body is at 45-degree angle

• Keeping body completely straight, pull yourself up by driving elbows back and rotating palms to face each other at top position

• Lower body with control and rotate palms so they face ground at start position

• Repeat for specified reps

4 SIDE LUNGE WITH OVERHEAD PRESS

Sistrunk: "This improves groin strength, which prevents pulls from lateral movements. Keep your knee behind your toes and drive through your heel. Your butt can go below knee level, but you must be under control. Everything should be in line from your wrist down when you press."

• Assume athletic stance and hold dumbbells at shoulder level, palms facing you

• Press dumbbells overhead while rotating palms away from you

• Lower dumbbells to start position, step right, and lower into side lunge position with knee behind toes and bring dumbbell between knees

• Drive back into start position

• Perform overhead press

• Repeat movement to left

5

SUPERMAN PUSH-UPS ON STRAPS

Sistrunk: "When Jimmy first did these, he was shaking. He's a lot stronger now, but you can still tell he's really working. This is for shoulder stability, chest and triceps; it's a core workout, too. If it's too difficult, just hold the top position. You'll feel your abs working."

• Assume push-up position on straps attached to pull-up bar

• Perform push-ups in controlled manner for specified reps

6

CABLE ROTATIONS WITH PHYSIOBALL

Sistrunk: "This is as close to hitting a ball as we can get. Let your core do the work; don't let your outside tricep kick out to help you. The physioball keeps pressure off your shoulders and keeps you honest with good form."

Rollins: "It's just like hitting, because you're standing and have to turn. Take that 50 pounds I was doing it with, then take that to a three-pound bat. How much stronger are you going to feel?"

• Assume athletic position with physioball against sternum and cable system to right

• Hold rope attachment with left hand on left side of physioball. Place open right hand over cable on right side of ball

• Keeping ball tight to chest, explosively rotate left and pivot on right foot, like you are swinging bat

• Pause, return to start position with control

• Repeat for specified reps

7 BACK EXTENSIONS

Sistrunk: "Everyone does crunches, but they need to work their back to balance things out. This helps posture and prevents injury from the constant rotating baseball players do. Before the body moves, tighten your glutes—then bring your body up."

- Assume position on back extension machine

- Lower upper body until waist is bent 90 degrees

- Fire glutes to raise upper body until in line with lower body

- Lower with control; repeat

8 SPRINTER CRUNCHES

Sistrunk: "Your abs stay engaged the whole time; keep them nice and tight. Don't just plop back down on the ground. This helps with form running and body control. This exercise can be performed with a medicine ball when the athlete has mastered this level."

- Lie on back with knees slightly bent and feet on floor

- Perform crunch and bring right knee to chest

- Hold position and pump arms in sprinting fashion three times

- Lower and perform motion with left leg

- Repeat in alternating fashion

HAMSTRING CURL VARIATIONS

Sistrunk: "I do this because so many athletes are quad-dominant from everything else they do. We need to balance them out. I believe in shocking the system by doing different things and giving it different demands. Most important is preventing hamstring pulls."

- Perform set of hamstring curls with both legs in controlled fashion

- Perform next set in single-leg fashion with lighter weight

- Perform next set by alternating legs each rep

- Perform final set as 10 reps with both legs, then 10 reps alternating legs

POST-WORKOUT STRETCH

1 STRADDLE STRETCH WITH PHYSIOBALL

- Sit on butt and spread legs wider than hip distance apart

- Bend at waist to reach both hands toward physioball, stretching to full range of motion to right, center, and left

2 ABDUCTOR GLUTE STRETCH

- Assume hurdler position on ground with left heel tucked into groin and right leg extended out and right

- Fold torso over toward left knee; hold

3 LOW BACK STRETCH

- Lie on back; hug knees into chest

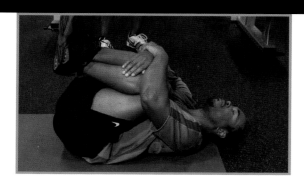

4 HAMSTRING

- Lie on back, with legs extended forward

- Position left foot over partner's shoulder, keeping leg straight

- Partner slowly pushes leg up to point of tension; hold 8–12 seconds

- After release, push against partner's hand for 4–6 seconds

5 GROIN/GLUTE

- Lie on back; bring one knee to chest

- Partner applies pressure by taking knee to side of body

6 LOW BACK/HAMSTRING STRETCH

- Lie on back; cross one leg over body

- Partner lifts leg toward opposite shoulder and applies pressure

MVP HITTING PROGRESSION

1 KNEELING SINGLE-ARM SOFT TOSS

Thompson: "We're trying to develop the proper path to the ball. Your front hand is your guide, and your top hand helps snap and explode through the ball—almost like having an axe in your hand and [swinging] to chop a tree. The movement is just from your elbow to your hand. Being on one knee helps you stay back on the ball and keep a good bat angle. Don't raise your elbow; you'll create a different path to the ball."

- Near plate, kneel on front knee and extend back leg so that foot is at back of batter's box

- Using front arm only, hold bat by back shoulder

- Partner will toss ball; hit ball by swinging with front arm in chopping motion

2 STANDING SINGLE-ARM SOFT TOSS

Thompson: "This is the next step of the progression. We have Jimmy stand up and hold the bat with two hands to give him the feeling of hitting."

- Assume batting stance at plate, holding bat with both hands

- As partner tosses ball, swing with front arm only in chopping motion to hit ball

FRONT TOSS

Thompson: "I can throw more strikes to him this way. He's just working on trying to get his swing again and get his hands ready. This is a controlled environment, so he can make sure to stay back, keep his balance and just let his hands flow through the ball."

- Assume batting stance at plate

- As partner tosses balls underhand from behind L-screen 20 feet away, take controlled swings with proper path to ball

LIVE BATTING PRACTICE

Thompson: "He's looking to drive the ball and hit line drives all over the field. This brings [together] all the elements we've been working on. Just try to get a nice path and let your hands drive the ball. [Rollins] told me he had a great season last year because he learned to catch the baseball with the bat right in front of him, not try to kill or lift it. That's what you are working [toward]."

Rollins: "Power is generated by bat speed. If you have a short, compact swing and your hands are close to your body, that's when you're strongest. If you hold the bat way out and have someone tap it, the bat will move. If you do the same thing with your hands in close, the bat won't move because you're stronger there. I have long arms for how short I am, so I scoot up on the plate to bring the ball closer to me."

- Assume batting stance at plate

- As partner pitches overhand from behind L-screen 45 feet away, take swings with proper path to ball

JIMMY ROLLINS' TRAINING GUIDE

DYNAMIC WARM-UP AND STRETCHING

EXERCISE	REPS/DISTANCE
Half-Speed Run	
High Knees	
Butt Kicks	
A-Skips	
Walking Lunge With Twist	Perform these drills down and back on a basketball court (20–30 yards each way) in continuous fashion
Straight-Leg March	
Walking Knee Pulls	
Toe Ups	
Walking Heel Pulls	
Shuffle With Lateral Lunge	

PARTNER STRETCH

EXERCISE	REPS	TIME
Straddle [Center, Right, Left]	2–3 each side	hold 10–15 seconds
Glute	2–3 each side	hold 10–15 seconds
Hip Abductor	2–3 each side	hold 10–15 seconds
Hamstring	2–3 each side	hold 10–15 seconds
Lying Trunk Twist	2–3 each side	hold 10–15 seconds

SPEED, AGILITY, AND POWER

EXERCISE	SETS	REPS/DISTANCE
Speed Lunges	4	30 yards
Falling Starts	4	30 yards
Resisted Starts	4	20 yards
Resisted Shuffle	4	20 yards
Overhead Med Ball Throws	4	10
Ground Balls on Speed Ladder With Med Ball		3 [Down and back is one rep]

STRENGTH

EXERCISE	SETS	REPS/DISTANCE
Dumbbell Squat Press	4	10
Kettlebell Swings	4	20 [10 each way]
Inverted Row on Straps	4	15–20
Side Lunge With Overhead Press	4	20 [10 each way]
Superman Push-Ups on Straps	4	10–15
Cable Rotations With Physioball	3	12 each side
Back Extensions	4	12–15
Sprinter Crunches	3	20–25
Hamstring Curl Variations	4	10–15

POST-WORKOUT STRETCH

MVP HITTING PROGRESSION

EXERCISE	SETS	REPS/TIME
Kneeling Single-Arm Soft Toss	1	30–40 swings at each side of plate
Standing Single-Arm Soft Toss	1	30–40 swings at each side of plate
Front Toss	1	50 swings at each side of plate
Live Batting Practice	3–4	15 minutes total

CHAPTER 8

JOHAN SANTANA

EDITOR'S NOTE

When we caught up with Johan Santana during spring training in 2007, he was the Minnesota Twins' undisputed ace and the most feared pitcher in baseball. The combination of his explosive fastball and embarrassment-inducing off-speed pitches kept opposing batters helpless in the box.

Until that point, Santana had been pretty quiet and private about his training and approach to the game, so we jumped at the opportunity to cover his preparation and workouts with Twins strength coach Perry Castellano.

Expecting a much lankier guy, we were caught off guard when meeting Santana. Instead of the long limbs and towering build of a prototypical major league pitcher, he possessed a 6-foot-tall, muscular—almost stocky—physique, with one of the widest sets of shoulders we'd ever seen. He looked more like an NFL running back than a league-leading strikeout artist.

Castellano had designed a workout specifically to embrace and enhance Santana's powerful build, increase his strength, and boost flexibility in his core and lower body. All together, the goal

JOHAN SANTANA CELEBRATES A COMPLETE-GAME VICTORY IN 2009. KEEPING HIS CORE STRONG HELPS PROTECT SANTANA'S PITCHING SHOULDER DURING THE SEASON.

was to protect the hurler's shoulder from the stress that would occur if his legs, hips, and core did not work properly.

Santana was quick to joke around and have some fun during our shoot; but when it was time to work, the smiles disappeared. He may even have hurled some light-hearted, but not-so-nice, comments Castellano's way when certain exercises were prescribed. In the end, though, the fireballer knew the workout was making him better.

Now at the age of 30, Santana and his fastball are still popping—the result of his solid training base. As the ace for the New York Mets, he has continued to post ERAs and W-L records among Major League Baseball's best.

This is the Johan Santana cover feature as it appeared in the May 2007 issue of *STACK* Magazine.

SMOKING ACE

Weary batters stand in against Johan Santana like dazed prizefighters— off balance, knowing that the knockout punch is on its way. No one ever knows a thing about the final blow, except that it will come from the left with Johan's signature on it. Will it be the exploding two-seam fastball, tailing away from the batter's reach? How about the biting slider bearing in on his hands? Or, could it be the mocking change-up that floats across the plate at a tantalizing 75 mph? Whatever pitch drops over the plate, chances are it will send the batter back to the dugout, finished off by the nastiest pitcher in baseball. Take a seat.

Things have improved for Johan Santana since his first experience on the diamond. Despite his talent, potential, and enthusiasm, the young pitcher was sent packing from his first baseball practice in his hometown of Tovar, Merida State, Venezuela. "I was just a kid who wanted to play baseball," Santana recalls. "That was the very first time I walked onto a baseball field. I decided to go with a friend, but I wasn't wearing any kind of baseball uniform—just shorts, a short-sleeved shirt and no socks or hat. The coach sent me home right away, telling me that if I wanted to play baseball, I had to look like a baseball player.

I felt bad, but I still had hope."

The following day, Santana put his baseball dreams back on track with the help of his father, a semi-pro baseball player. "I went back home and started looking for the smallest jersey I could find in my dad's uniform collection," Santana says. "Even though it was way too big, because I was only 11 years old, I wore it the next day. It's funny how everything started for me." Once the coach realized who his father was, the coach immediately changed how he treated Santana.

Following in his father's footsteps, Santana took to shortstop. "I used to watch my dad play and practice at shortstop," Santana says. "My brother and I would go up to the baseball field with him, and I wanted to be just like him, because he was my idol. I used to wear his glove and try to do things just like him. Since I was using his glove, I was throwing righty. It wasn't until later that I realized it was much easier for me to throw with my left hand." This revelation, coupled with his pure athleticism, made Santana a mainstay in centerfield for his Little League team. However, Santana's pure throwing power couldn't be ignored; it eventually made him a natural selection for the mound.

"At first, it was all about my arm strength, but then I started learning the mechanics of pitching and put in a lot of hard work," Santana says. "I was patient with myself, my training and practice, so I could become a better player."

Santana didn't pitch in his first organized game until his early teens. But when he finally took to the rubber, his ability and improvements were undeniable. His team—the Chiquilines—played in Venezuela's national baseball tournament each year, providing Santana the opportunity to show people his pitching prowess. Soon, major league scouts were making the treacherous 10-hour drive through the Andes Mountains to watch the Venezuelan strikeout artist.

"It was a great feeling to have all of those scouts interested and coming to watch me play—and I was surprised by it," Santana says. "I didn't even know what a scout looked like at the time. I always had that dream and thought about it. But at the same time, I thought it might be out of reach, because there weren't many baseball players from where I grew up, mostly soccer players. But the things scouts were saying to me made me think, 'Wow, I can do this.'"

One particular scout, the Astros' Andres Reiner, knew immediately that Santana had

major league–caliber talent, and he brought the word back to the organization. Soon thereafter, Santana signed with Houston and spent the 1999 season in their minor-league system. However, by not including Santana on their 40-man roster at the end of the year, the Astros gave the Marlins an opportunity to snag him in the Rule 5 Draft. An immediate player swap then sent him to the Twins. The young, raw pitcher had found the perfect place to grow and develop.

During the 2000 season, Santana went from Rule 5 selection to bullpen specialist for the Twins. Santana earned his first big league victory against the team that had let him go. "That was a very memorable moment for me," Santana says. "My first win happened to come against Houston—the team I never got to play for in the majors, because they released me. It was special, so I framed the scorecard and hung it on the wall at my mother's house. It's still there."

In 2002, his third season in the Majors, Santana made it clear that such a sweet payback was only the beginning of bigger things to come. His workmanlike contribution helped the Twins go from likely contraction casualty to pennant contender. He put together a record of 8–6 with a 2.99 ERA; but more impressive were Santana's 137 Ks in just 100 innings of action, which helped him realize how dominating he could become and fueled his intense desire to crack the Twins' starting rotation.

Santana finally got his wish in July 2003. "Man, that was great—finally being able to go out and start," he says. "All the hard work over the years paid off, and I was able to show everyone what I could do." Santana demonstrated this in a historic fashion. He went a perfect 8–0 down the stretch for a final record of 12–3, with a 3.07 ERA and 169 Ks. The Twins had found their ace.

Some analysts expected Santana's steady improvement to plateau, but the 25-year-old's game was just coming around. In 2004, Santana put together one of the best seasons by a pitcher on record. Routinely, he made the best hitters look silly at the plate by setting them up with one pitch and finishing them off with another. Santana was nailing his spots—better than any other pitcher in baseball. His fastball was no longer just 95 mph down the middle; its natural

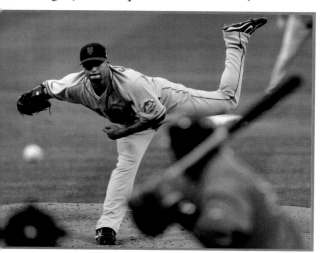

movement found the edges of the plate, making it even more lethal. He also gained more control of his slider and more confidence in his change-up. Santana learned to deliver his slow ball so that it looked identical to his fastball, even though it was crossing the plate 20 mph slower. Most pitchers can only hope for a 10- to 12-mph difference. Santana says: "I want [all of my pitches] to look the same, with the same delivery and same release point, so the hitter will think it's the same pitch every time—even though it will have a different velocity or spin."

Santana's breakout performance resulted in the best pitching numbers in the majors, effectively proving he was the finest pitcher in the world. In the second half of the season, he went 13–0 with an ethereal ERA of 1.18. Coming through in the clutch, Santana was especially hot in the always-important month of August, when he gave up only 10 earned runs and struck out 52. His stellar play and season record of 20–6 propelled the Twins to the AL Central Championship by a nine-game margin. Garnering all 28 first-place votes, Santana won the American League's Cy Young Award.

Santana's outstanding numbers and success continued over the next two seasons. In 2006, he took home another Cy Young and won the Triple Crown of pitching by leading the majors in ERA, strikeouts, and wins—the first pitcher to do so since Dwight Gooden in '85 and Sandy Koufax in '66 before that. There was no end in sight for Santana's domination. And while most major league pitchers are known for one, or at most two, trademark pitches, Santana continues to refine his control and perfect his mastery over three untouchable variations. Added to his physical ability are Santana's confidence and attacking strategy on the mound. "I'm very aggressive even though I might not look like it when I'm pitching," he says. "I'm not scared to throw my pitches and go out there and do my job."

"This is hurting me, Diablo! You are crazy!"

This is the third time in an hour that Santana has called Twins strength and conditioning coordinator Perry Castellano "El Diablo." "He calls me that quite often. Sometimes he'll call me Mr. Perry if we're not working him this hard," Castellano says.

Although Santana's feeling some serious muscle burn, he recognizes the humor and irony behind his comment. Castellano and his training are not hurting him; in fact, they are keeping Santana healthy. "I must protect the starting pitcher. That is the number one goal with Johan," Castellano says. "Out of every 170 guys that a team signs, only seven get a cup of coffee in the big leagues. So a guy like Santana, to do the things he's doing, he has a gift. And it's my job to protect that gift."

Santana echoes Castellano's sentiment. "My main focus is to remain healthy throughout the entire season," he says. "I know that if I'm healthy, I will have a great chance to perform very well. That is why everything I do is based around keeping my body healthy. You can tell right away when things start to break down, because it really affects your pitching."

Pat Santana on the back or shake his hand, and you immediately notice his "gift." Castellano says, "He's got incredible natural shoulder size and tremendous strength on the left side of his body. You can feel how developed he is right away. At six feet tall, he really shouldn't be able to throw as hard as he can. Most pitchers at this level are well over that height with very long levers. He can produce that velocity because he's so strong through his core and powerful in his legs."

To protect Santana and provide a safe environment for his gift, Castellano has created a program that steers clear of size-based improvements. Instead, he uses ground-based exercises to help Santana develop his flexibility, strength, balance, and core strength and stability. "Power and strength are not size," Castellano says. "And putting on size would only hurt Santana. We want to improve his low back and ab strength, and condition his lower body to overcome fatigue. When a pitcher loses his legs, everything begins to break down, which puts a lot of stress on his shoulder."

Since working with Castellano, Santana's game has experienced positive effects. "You have to be strong to pitch—and stay that way throughout the year," says Santana. "Because of this training, I can feel my strength in the middle of the season, even at the end."

A starting pitcher's training is the most clear-cut and defined in baseball, because everyone knows when he has to perform on the mound. Given the Twins' five-day rotation, Castellano plans Santana's workout for his four non-pitching days. Since Santana is at a level where he knows exactly what his body needs, he is given some flexibility as to how to get the work done.

Day 1: Lower body strength
Day 2: Bullpen power day, jump rope, and upper body strength
Day 3: Bullpen touch and feel, lower body circuit, and balance drills
Day 4: Med ball abs, conditioning [Santana chooses to shag fly balls during batting practice]

Day 1 is Santana's most intense day, and it's when the most progress occurs. The following exercises comprise the Cy Young winner's Day 1 training.

MOVEMENT PREP

SCIFIT PRO II WARM UP

Castellano: "This is a total-body warm-up to get his blood flowing before we move on to weights and other exercises."

- Perform upper body and lower body rotations on SciFit Pro II machine

- Alternate 15 seconds of intense speed with 15 seconds of slower speed; change direction of movement every 60 seconds

Alternative: Elliptical machine

ANKLE BAND ROUTINE

Attach small band around ankles, then assume athletic stance. Perform the following drills for 10 paces with each leg.

Castellano: "These exercises strengthen the hip flexors and core, including the low back, which is necessary for baseball. We build from the ground up by working the triple extension of the ankle, knee, and hip, which is just like a pitcher's movement when he stands tall and then pushes off with one leg. I liken this and the pitching motion to getting out of a car; you get upright then push out all at once. A lot of things have to happen simultaneously."

Johan: "I hate this. Look at me; I can barely walk when I'm done."

Benefits: Glute, hip, and leg strength and endurance

1 STRAIGHT AHEAD

- Step forward and 45 degrees right with right foot; repeat with left foot, but step left. Repeat set backwards.

2 LATERAL STEPOVERS

- Move laterally left by raising left leg up, over, and out. Bring right leg up and over, then set it down next to left foot. Repeat set in opposite direction.

3 CARIOCA

- Cross trail foot in front then behind lead foot. Repeat set in opposite direction.

4 GROUND BALLS

- Perform Straight Ahead movement; but after each pace, bring feet to even stance, squat down, then reach to ground like you are fielding a ball; repeat backwards

HURDLE MOBILITY

Perform the following exercises over five consecutive hurdles.

Castellano: "This is also like the pitching motion. Because much of the pitching motion is on one leg, balance is necessary. This works hip flexibility with balance as an added component."

Benefits: Improved balance, hip flexibility, and coordination

1 FORWARD/BACKWARD

- Step over first hurdle with left leg; then in one movement, bring right leg over first and second hurdles. Continue pattern.

2 LATERAL

- Stand with row of hurdles to left. Step over first hurdle with left leg, then right leg. Continue pattern. Repeat in opposite direction.

LATERAL KICKS

- With row of hurdles to your right and slightly in front of you, kick right leg over first hurdle, then left leg. Continue pattern. Repeat in opposite direction.

OVER-UNDERS

- Stand with row of alternating high and low hurdles to your right. Step over first low hurdle with left leg, then right leg. Then step under and through second hurdle with right leg as you squat down; step left leg through second hurdle. Repeat over-under pattern down length of hurdles.

MED BALL CORE ROUTINE

Perform the following exercises with an eight-pound med ball.

Castellano: "We start simple, then get more complex with each exercise in this routine. We work the entire core—including the lower back—in every direction, especially with rotational movements. I like to have Johan standing in a weight-bearing position, because that's how he pitches."

Johan: "I hate the Russian Twist; it's the hardest. But I like the Rotation Throws, because I get to throw the ball back at Mr. Perry very hard."

1 MED BALL SIT-UP WITH TOSS

- As partner tosses ball to you, perform sit-up and throw ball back to partner

2 RUSSIAN TWIST WITH TOSS

- Sit on ground, cross ankles and elevate feet

- When partner tosses ball, catch it, and rotate right, then left so ball touches ground just outside of hips

- Throw ball back to partner

3 SPLIT-STANCE ROTATIONAL MED BALL THROW

- Get in split stance, left foot forward

- As partner throws ball from left, catch it, rotate left, and throw it back

- Repeat with left leg forward and partner on right, then right leg forward with partner on right, then right leg forward with partner on left

4 REACTIVE MED BALL SIT-UPS

- With partner in front of you and placing his hands at different locations above you, perform sit-ups and touch med ball to partner's hands

STRENGTH TRAINING

1 LEG PRESS

Castellano: "Growing up in Venezuela, Johan didn't have the proper equipment to squat. So I don't want to load his back up with a bar, which is why we avoid squatting."

- Assume position on leg press machine with feet slightly wider than hip distance and toes pointing out slightly

- Lower weight sled with control until knees are bent 90 degrees

- Drive weight up by extending legs to start position

Benefits: Lower body strength and power

2 LEG CURL

Castellano: "The leg curl and extension are how we make sure muscles in the lower body, above the knee joint, are balanced."

- Assume position on leg curl machine

- Contract hamstrings to bring heels to butt

- Lower weight with control; repeat

Benefits: Hamstring strength and muscle balance

LEG EXTENSION

- Assume position on leg extension machine

- Raise weight until legs are fully extended

- Lower weight with control until knees are bent almost 90 degrees; repeat

Benefits: Quad strength and muscle balance

SEATED CALF RAISE

Castellano: "This is one of the few times we isolate a muscle."

- Assume position on seated calf raise machine

- Drive weight up by extending ankles

Benefits: Lower-leg strength and improved push off the mound

FLEXIBILITY

PARTNER STRETCH

Have partner bring each of the following stretches to point of tension, then hold for 10 seconds.

Castellano: "A partner can get you to a point you can't get to yourself. I can feel right away if Johan is tight in one muscle or on one side, so there is a benefit to having someone stretch you."

1 HAMSTRING

2 GLUTE/INTERNAL ROTATION

3 LOW BACK

4 GROIN

A CONSTANT CYCLE

Castellano's protective philosophy doesn't just govern weight room work on Johan's non-pitching days. It's a full-time mindset. "The moment Johan comes out of a game, he starts getting his body ready for the next start," Castellano says. "He does a cool down activity immediately for about 10 to 12 minutes—with a stationary bike or a slide board. This helps him get some fresh blood moving; and then he ices." Johan adds, "I do everything possible to take care of myself and recover, beginning the moment after I pitch."

JOHAN SANTANA'S TRAINING GUIDE

MOVEMENT PREP	SETS	
SciFit Pro II Warm Up	Alternate 15 seconds of intense speed with 15 seconds of slower speed. Change direction of movement every 60 seconds	

ANKLE BAND ROUTINE	SETS	REPS
Straight-Ahead	1	10 paces each leg
Lateral Stepovers	1	10 paces each leg
Carioca	1	10 paces each leg
Ground Balls	1	10 paces each leg

HURDLE MOBILITY	REPS
Forward/Backward	5 consecutive hurdles each direction
Lateral	5 consecutive hurdles each direction
Lateral Kicks	5 consecutive hurdles each direction
Over-Unders	5 consecutive hurdles each direction

MED BALL CORE ROUTINE	SETS	REPS
Med Ball Sit-Up With Toss	1	12
Russian Twist With Toss	1	12
Split-Stance Rotational Med Ball Throw	1	12 each way
Reactive Med Ball Sit-Ups	1	20

STRENGTH TRAINING	SETS	REPS	REST
Leg Press	3	10	45 seconds
Leg Curl	2	10	45 seconds
Leg Extension	2	10	45 seconds
Seated Calf Raise	2	10	45 seconds

FLEXIBILITY	REPS	DURATION
Hamstring	1 each leg	with partner; hold 10 sec
Glute/Internal Rotation	1 each leg	with partner; hold 10 sec
Low Back	1 each leg	with partner; hold 10 sec
Groin	1 each leg	with partner; hold 10 sec

CHAPTER 9

JUSTIN MORNEAU

EDITOR'S NOTE

After just his second full season in the major leagues, Justin Morneau took home the 2006 AL MVP Award. The 6'4" first baseman belted 30 homers, drove in 130 runs and hit over .320. But despite these impressive stats, Morneau was mostly unknown outside of Minnesota, and his MVP title left many baseball fans wondering, "Who is this guy?"

During the following off-season, we set out to answer the question, which required a January trip to Morneau's hometown of Vancouver, Canada. Knowing the young star's history as a standout high school hockey player, we were not surprised that he worked to take his game to the next level at Vancouver-based Twist Conditioning, owned by Peter Twist, the former NHL strength coach and elite performance expert.

During our full day of interaction with Morneau, we witnessed an intense training session that included speed, agility, core, and strength work—all of which incorporated a specific "Twist." We also walked away knowing who Morneau is—a talented, dedicated athlete who's earned everything he's won.

JUSTIN MORNEAU ROUNDS THE BASES AFTER A HOME RUN IN 2009. MORNEAU INCORPORATES HIS OTHER LOVE—HOCKEY—INTO HIS BASEBALL TRAINING.

Inspired by the young slugger's determination, we awarded him the cover of our magazine. This is the Justin Morneau cover feature as it originally appeared in the March 2007 issue of *STACK* Magazine.

AGAINST THE GRAIN

Justin Morneau sacrificed his high school social life for baseball. Some people might say he missed out on the best years of his life. Others might think that limiting his social life was a hefty price to pay for a shot at the pros. Morneau is not one of those people.

From the beginning, Morneau was destined to do two things: play hockey and play baseball. Hockey was a given for this naturally athletic Canadian. Baseball, though, was not, as the game lacks the puck's popularity up north—especially for a guy of Justin's stature [6'4", 225-pound].

Thank God popularity never fueled Morneau's passion. Instead, he found inspiration elsewhere, starting with his parents. His father, who played baseball in his youth, served as Justin's hitting coach until he was 16. Responsible for his left-handed swing is Morneau's mom, who was an accomplished fast-pitch softball player when she was younger.

Other influencing factors in Justin's choice to play ball were fellow Canadian Larry Walker and the Toronto Blue Jays. Walker starred in the outfield for the Montreal Expos from 1989 to 1994. In 1995, he was traded to the Colorado Rockies, and two years later he took home the National League MVP award—the first Canadian to score the honor.

In 1992 and 1993, when Justin was in his formative years as an 11- and 12-year-old, the Jays won back-to-back World Series Championships, with John Olerud as their first baseman. "John Olerud was one of my favorites. Obviously Larry Walker, too, but I'd pretend to be [Olerud] a lot when we played whiffle ball in the backyard," Morneau says. "I tried to swing like him. I've looked at videos, and our swings are pretty similar."

Justin transitioned from a dual- to a single-sport athlete when he was 16, simply by turning down an invitation to training camp for a Canadian Junior Hockey Team. "I had a pretty good summer playing baseball, so I decided to not go to the training camp," he says. "They called me a couple times to ask and make sure that I didn't want to play hockey. That's when I knew what I wanted to do."

His decision to forgo a possible career in his country's beloved sport quickly proved to be the right one. In 1999, two years after Morneau ditched the skates, the Minnesota Twins drafted him out of high school in the third round. By 2003, he worked his way through the

farm system to make his major league debut. Morneau's true talent shined in 2006, only one year after he completed his first full major league season. He powered up at the plate for 34 homeruns, 130 RBIs, and a .321 batting average. Following in the footsteps of one of his childhood idols, Morneau earned his league's MVP title.

Despite his huge accomplishments in America's favorite pastime, Morneau gets little attention in his Canadian hometown. "Baseball is not even close to being on the same scale as hockey," he says. "I can go pretty much anywhere in Vancouver and not be recognized." And although he doesn't get the fame or prestige of a pro hockey player, Morneau has no regrets about choosing baseball; it's the sport he was always most dedicated to. "I worked hard at baseball," he says. "I set up my high school schedule so I didn't have class during the middle of the day so I could get to the batting cages. I'd be the only one in there hitting as

much as I wanted for hours at a time."

More than just his class schedule, Justin centered every aspect of his high school life around baseball. He looked beyond the season and into the future, so he could be the best baseball player today, tomorrow and in the future, when he'd have a pro career. He says, "I always did stuff a little different. I'd always be the first one to the park and the last one to leave. Everything revolved around what I was going to do in baseball for that day; it's all that mattered. I didn't think about anything else. My friends would go hang out late at night, but I never did that in high school. I always had a game or practice the next day I'd be thinking about. So when they were out late, I'd be home watching TV or sleeping."

Setting Justin even further apart from the typical high school kid, he never considered it a sacrifice to stay home instead of hanging with friends. Justin was doing what he wanted to do and what was necessary to make a career out of the game he loves. "In the winter, I'd be in

the batting cages blocking balls for half an hour at a time, then I'd hit until my hands bled," he says. "But I don't really consider those things a sacrifice. That was fun for me, and that was what I loved doing. It's what I needed to do. There were times I'd look around at all my friends who were going out, and I'd just be playing baseball all the time. I look back now and realize it was completely worth it because I get to do what I love for a living."

Fully dedicating himself to becoming the best player possible would allow Morneau to walk away from the game—whether he made it to the pros or not—with no regrets. "Even if you don't make it to the bigs, you should work hard so you can look back and know you tried as hard as you could," he says. "Sometimes you just don't have enough talent, but it's a lot easier to live with that than to have to look back and say, 'I wish I would have done this or that.'"

Morneau has continued working hard through every off-season. To really take his game to the next level, he is training at Twist

Conditioning, working with strength coaches Peter Twist [president and CEO], Miki Kawahara [manager of baseball conditioning] and Dean Shiels [vice president of athlete conditioning]. Along with the rest of the Twist staff, these three coaches oversee every aspect of Justin's training to ensure that he'll be ready for another season of dominating MVP-type numbers.

Maybe one day, Morneau's stellar play will convert some of Vancouver's hockey faithful into diehard baseball fans—or at least Justin Morneau fans.

Oh, Canada

The way Twist, Kawahara, and Shiels were moving purposely around their weight room on this Thursday morning, you'd think an entire baseball team was coming in to train. But when 10:45 hit the clock, just four men entered the facility. Not just any four men, though; they are four of Canada's best products: Baltimore Orioles pitcher Adam Loewen and outfielder Adam Stern, New York Yankees outfielder Aaron Guiel and, of course, Morneau—all of whom played on the Canadian National Team that beat the USA in the 2006 World Baseball Classic. While this foursome makes up Twist's first batch of professional baseball clients, the Vancouver-based group has trained nearly 700 professional athletes, including hockey, soccer, and football players.

Using a three or four coach-to-player ratio, the Twist training staff can tailor workouts specific to each athlete's individual needs, then work hands-on to execute the program. For Morneau, the training focuses on improving his already-existing strengths. "Everyone knows Justin and what his forte is; he's a smart athlete who can hit the ball well," Twist says. "For him, at the end of the day, he needs power. And since Justin is a go-to player, we're concerned with him in terms of durability. We want him to handle high volume so he can stay in the game."

Kawahara echoes Twist's point, adding that rotary power will help Morneau translate his strength into greater pop at the plate. "We know how powerful Justin is," Kawahara says. "But if we teach him how to link his legs, and especially his core, into his rotary movements more, he will transfer power more efficiently."

After a thorough warm-up, the players' workouts call for standing core work, shoulder strength, weight training, and finally, floor core work. Each segment and the exercises within train both the muscles and nervous system for maximum results. Twist says, "I use a computer as an analogy: Most training works on the hard drive, so we do that a lot. However, we also want to work on the software so it's smarter. So we train the muscles and the neural system to produce an athlete who is not only stronger, but also more skillful and a better overall athlete."

Although all four players' workouts integrate the same segments, the exercises included are slightly different based on the demands of their positions. While the two outfielders focus a bit more on acceleration to help them cover their region of the field, and the pitcher concentrates on shoulder stability with less rest between sets to mimic the demands of a day on the mound, Justin works more lateral movements to replicate what he does at his post on first base.

Justin's massive workout, which is part of a four-days-a-week training plan, takes more than two hours to complete from start to finish. Check out one of his complete weight-training complexes as well as a sample of exercises from the segments included in this particular day's workout.

WARM-UP

To get his blood flowing and his body prepared for the more intense part of his workout, Justin starts with a dynamic warm-up. The coaches at Twist prescribe five to seven multi-directional movements through a series of cones set up in a zigzag pattern. Besides preventing the boredom associated with simple down-and-back, linear patterns, "the zigzag allows you to do things you can't do as well in a linear warm-up, like plants, cuts and changes of direction," Kawahara says. After the zigzag drills, Justin works on quick feet, coordination, and the ability to plant, change direction, and balance through the speed ladder.

WALKING LUNGE WITH ROTATION

Kawahara: We employ the Walking Lunge With Rotation toward the end of the dynamic warm-up to put the muscles through the range of motion they'll be experiencing during the workout. The lunge gets a nice, long stretch for the hip flexors and works the glutes and hamstrings. The rotation gets the lower back warmed up without too much force or weight.

- Set up six cones five to seven yards apart in zigzag pattern

- Step into lunge in direction of first cone; drop hips until back knee is one to two inches off ground

- Rotate upper body with arms at shoulder level to same side as forward leg

- Step forward with opposite leg; repeat

- Continue pattern moving from cone to cone

COACHING POINTS

▶ Make sure to hold at bottom of lunge for two seconds

▶ Keep arms at shoulder level

▶ Cycle leg out as far as possible with each step and drop hips into lunge

ICKEY SHUFFLE STICK

Kawahara: We're working on single-leg stability and balance on the outside, which is so important for hitting and throwing foot work. We're also making Justin quicker and more explosive off his outside foot by holding and then driving off that foot into the next square. This transfers well for him as a first baseman, since he needs short, quick footwork to make outside turns or inside pivots for a throw to second.

- Move through speed ladder with a two-feet-in, one-foot-out pattern: right foot in, left foot in; right foot out to right side; pause on right foot for one count

- Explosively drive off right foot and step left foot forward into second square, followed by right foot in same square; left foot out to left side; pause on left foot for one count

- Continue pattern entire length of ladder

COACHING POINTS

- ➡ Move through ladder with speed, but under control
- ➡ Keep head up and facing forward
- ➡ Move arms for momentum

Twist: The majority of our core work is done standing to work on stability and rotation. We integrate movement into the drills so the athletes have to activate their core during the movement, not just when they're static.

ISOMETRIC HOCKEY STICK HOLD

Kawahara: As you start switching your feet, really focus on keeping the same amount of pressure through the rack.

- Stand holding hockey stick with hands 18 inches apart and legs split, front to back

- Press end of hockey stick against squat rack at waist height

- Hold position for 10 seconds keeping constant pressure

- Continue applying pressure for 10 additional seconds, but continually switching feet placement, front to back

- Repeat for opposite side

COACHING POINTS

➤ Keep pressure on stick at all times
➤ Stay controlled when switching feet

PARTNER PHYSIOBALL HOLD AND PUSH

Kawahara: This drill relates to being stronger at contact when hitting. You'll be able to accelerate through the baseball, rather than lose speed on the bat when you hit it.

- In athletic stance, hold physioball with arms bent at chest level

- Facing you, partner stands with feet together and one arm extended, touching physioball

- Partner pushes physioball five times with left hand, then five times with right

- Resist partner's pushes, holding physioball in place

- Switch to standing with feet together and hand touching physioball, while partner resists you pushing

- Next set, partner holding ball chops feet laterally, with out-out-in-in pattern, while keeping ball stationary

COACHING POINTS

- Focus on keeping core tight
- Do not allow physioball to move in any direction

ROTATOR CUFF WORK

Justin performs several drills to strengthen and condition his rotator cuffs, which protect his shoulders from the wear and tear of the 162-game season. "Over an entire season, he throws a lot, so muscular endurance in the shoulders is very important," Kawahara says.

To accomplish this, Justin performs 2 sets of 12–15 reps, using only a 2½-pound weight in each hand. He performs most of the drills lying face down on an incline bench, so he can fully extend his arms without his hands touching the floor and work his full ranges of motion.

1 PRONE L

- Lie face down on incline bench

- Hold 2½-pound weight in each hand with arms extended toward floor

- Pinching shoulder blades together, raise elbows to shoulder height with 90-degree bend in arm and forearms pointed toward floor

- Maintain 90-degree bend as you rotate hands toward ceiling

- Rotate hands back toward floor and return arms to starting position

COACHING POINT

➤ Focus on keeping 90-degree bend at elbow

2 PRONE Y

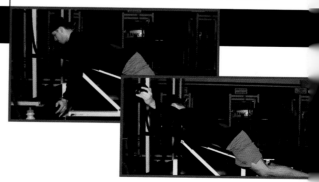

- Lie face down on incline bench

- Hold 2½-pound weight in each hand with arms extended toward floor

- Raise both arms toward ceiling at 45-degree angle, thumbs pointing up

- Keeping arms fully extended, return to starting position

COACHING POINT

➤ Keep arms fully extended and stay facing forward at all times

WEIGHT TRAINING COMPLEX

Training days include two complexes, each consisting of five to six lifts performed one after another with no rest. Once Justin completes one set of each lift, he takes a break, then starts over. He performs three sets of the first complex, then moves on to the second. "We use the complexes to tie the body together and overload the nervous system," Shiel says. "We want to challenge the muscles and the mind."

Justin's workout on this day incorporated two full-body complexes, rather than one focused on either his upper or lower body. This is because he missed a day of training due to travel. The first complex included exercises that work more of the major muscle groups and prime movers of the body. The second focused on more explosive movements and smaller muscle groups. Here is a breakdown of the second complex.

ROTARY SLED PULL

- Stand holding strap attached to weight sled to right

- Lower hips into quarter squat and rotate hips slightly toward sled

- Drag sled forward by exploding out of squat and rotating hips and upper body left, with arms extended at chest level

- Repeat with sled to opposite side

COACHING POINTS

➡ Focus on synchronizing rotating hips when exploding out of squat

➡ Fully extend back leg when rotating up

2 MED BALL TOSS

Kawahara: We package the Med Ball Toss with the Rotary Sled Pull because both focus on tying the lower and upper body together while working the core. The Sled Pull is a little slower with heavier weight, which leads well into the Med Ball Toss, allowing that to be really explosive. Justin can let go of the med ball as he drives off the backside.

- Stand in athletic stance with partner 10–15 feet to your left

- Catch med ball from partner, squat, and rotate right

- Twist and drive off both legs and use one hand to shot put med ball back to partner

- Release med ball at 45-degree angle

COACHING POINTS

- Focus on synchronizing rotating hips when exploding out of squat
- Fully extend back leg when rotating up
- Keep med ball at chest level when rotating to squat

3 PHYSIOBALL SINGLE-ARM DUMBBELL BENCH PRESS

Kawahara: This is similar to a lot of regular chest presses, but Justin finishes with a reach so he is able to get more range of motion and engage the core more with that pause. It also works on some rotation and stability because he's on the physioball.

- Lie with upper back on physioball, holding dumbbell in one hand

- Keeping feet flat on floor and hips up, press dumbbell from chest until arm is fully extended

- Reach dumbbell up as far as possible; hold for two counts

- Return dumbbell to chest; repeat for opposite arm

COACHING POINTS

- Keep core tight
- Reach dumbbell up as far as possible
- Keep knees bent 90 degrees

4 BUNGEE STRAIGHT ARM FLY

Shiel: Because Justin is standing, this drill works the pec and core simultaneously.

- Stand with right hand holding bungee cord, which is attached to top of squat rack to your right

- With arm fully extended to right and hand slightly above shoulder level, pull arm across body to opposite hip

- Control arm back to starting position

- Repeat for opposite side

COACHING POINTS

- ➧ **Keep arm fully extended at all times**
- ➧ **Control movement across body**

5 BUNGEE LATERAL EXTENSION

- Stand with left hand holding bungee cord, which is attached to top of squat rack to your right

- With arm extended across body at shoulder level and palm facing body, pull hand to left until it is 1–2 feet away from left hip and palm faces away from body

- Control arm back to starting position

- Repeat on opposite side

COACHING POINTS

- ➧ **Keep arm fully extended at all times**
- ➧ **Control movement across body**

CORE WORK

This batch of core work is focused on strength development and is aimed at overcoming weaknesses and incorporating more baseball-specific movements—in contrast with the previous core exercises, which are more suitable for a warm-up.

1 FOOT HARNESS SIDE-TO-SIDE KNEE TUCK

Kawahara: Because Justin's feet are supported, he's working shoulder stability in addition to his core. With the knee tuck, we're really trying to engage his lower abs and work his hip flexors. We want him to squeeze and pause at the top, then slowly control his legs back, which really overloads the core and develops good strength.

- Place feet in harnesses attached to cords hanging from top of squat rack

- Start in push-up position with left hand slightly farther up than right

- Pull knees up to side of chest and toward left arm

- Slowly control legs back to starting position

- Switch hand placements; repeat to opposite side

COACHING POINTS

➡ Control movements throughout exercise

➡ Tighten core when bringing knees to chest

2 BOSU MED BALL SUITCASE CRUNCH

Kawahara: Because the Bosu is dome-shaped, it exaggerates any movement Justin makes; he can tip off or lose his balance very easily. So, he has to be a lot more reactionary—by reading and responding to the environment, which really works his core. The dome forces him to work his upper abs to keep his back from rounding over the Bosu and his lower abs to keep his hips up, so he's working very hard before he even starts the crunch.

- Lie face-up with Bosu under lower back

- Keep shoulders and feet off ground

- Hold 2- to 4-pound medicine ball in each hand with arms extended overhead

- Perform crunch while pulling knees toward chest and bringing med ball toward knees

COACHING POINTS

➡ Keep feet and shoulders off ground

➡ Keep core tight

JUSTIN MORNEAU'S TRAINING GUIDE

WARM-UP	REPS	REST
Walking Lunge With Rotation	2	walk back between sets
Ickey Shuffle Stick	4 (twice with stick)	walk back between sets

CORE PREP	SETS	REPS/DURATION	REST
Isometric Hockey Stick Hold	2 each side	20 seconds	30–45 seconds
Partner Physioball Hold and Push	2	5 each direction	30–45 seconds

ROTATOR CUFF WORK	SETS	REPS	REST
Prone L	2	12–15	30 seconds
Prone Y	2	12–15	30 seconds

WEIGHT ROOM TRAINING COMPLEX	SETS	REPS
Rotary Sled Pull	3	8 each side
Med Ball Toss	3	8 each side
Physioball Dumbbell Bench Press	3	8 each arm
Bungee Straight Arm Fly	3	8 each side
Bungee Lateral Extension	3	8 each side

Superset all lifts; rest 60–90 seconds, then repeat complex from beginning.

CORE WORK	SETS	REPS	REST
Foot Harness Side-to-Side Knee Tuck	2	10 each side	60–75 seconds
Bosu Med Ball Suitcase Crunch	2	8 each side	60–75 seconds

CHAPTER 10

DAVID
WRIGHT

EDITOR'S NOTE

In an era when many athletes, particularly baseball players, are heavily criticized for what they do on and off the field, David Wright remains unscathed. Although he's the star of the Mets and a virtual king in the Big Apple, Wright refuses to let any area of his game or personal life go unchecked. Whether offering up substantial amounts of his time to the David Wright Foundation, an organization he founded to help kids with multiple sclerosis, or putting in extra work on the diamond, Wright continues to seek perfection by doing everything right.

Wright's baseball ability and status as a role model made it a no-brainer for us to feature him on the cover of *STACK* Magazine. When the opportunity arose, however, we were somewhat skeptical of his all-around greatness. At the start of the project, we admittedly had a "this-guy-is-probably-too-good-to-be-true" mindset. But we soon learned that the hype was all true. After spending a day with the perennial All-Star during 2009 spring training, we concluded that Wright was as polite and gracious off the field as he was talented and relentless on it—a man living up to his legend.

DAVID WRIGHT TAKES A CUT DURING A GAME IN 2009. WRIGHT'S ALL-AROUND GAME IS HONED THROUGH RIGOROUS ON-FIELD WORKOUTS AND PRACTICE.

After our meeting, Wright continued his success in the 2009 season. His consummate work ethic will undoubtedly keep the Mets championship contenders until he hangs up the leather.

This is the David Wright cover feature as it originally appeared in the April/May 2009 issue of *STACK* Magazine.

NEVER ENOUGH

David Wright doesn't fear failure, he absolutely despises it with a passion. In fact, most everything he has accomplished in the sport of baseball and in life has been driven by his hatred for the mere possibility of coming up short.

David Wright showed up almost 20 minutes early for his STACK cover shoot. He arrived with a smile and politely introduced himself. He answered all of our questions flawlessly and then took the diamond for an on-field spring training session. He stopped every ground ball, accurately pegged every throw, and took several perfect, beautiful, punishing swings at the plate. The young All-Star third baseman for the New York Mets is amazingly good at everything. But that's hardly enough for the Major League Baseball star.

Wright has earned three consecutive All-Star selections, two consecutive Gold Glove Awards, and two consecutive Silver Slugger Awards. He wields a .309 career batting average frosted with 130 homers and 489 RBI. Most MLB players would give anything for a stat line this impressive, but Wright is left unsatisfied. "I'm very tough on myself at times," he says. "I'm very pessimistic when it comes to evaluating my game. I always feel like there's room for improvement and that I'm not good enough. I think that continues to fuel the fire and makes sure that in the off-season I put myself in position to be the best player I can. That's the kind of attitude that I want to keep."

Wright's disgust for underachieving is so strong that the imperfect nature of baseball literally torments him. "The hardest thing for me to overcome is the amount of failure that comes along with playing this game," he says. "To be one of the best hitters in the game, you fail seven out of 10 times. You have to deal with that mentally and become mentally tough, where if you start struggling you can snap out of it by working."

The obsessive quest for perfection in an imperfect game began back in Virginia at Hickory High School, where Wright had dreams of playing ACC baseball. "I always knew that I had to outwork my competition, because I'm not a guy who had the best tools or the best skills," he says. "My parents taught me that work ethic where you might not be the best

player on the field, but you want to go out there and outwork everyone out on the field. That's the same philosophy I have now. I might not have the skill set, but I am going to put in the time and reach my potential."

Wright's fierce drive on the diamond allowed him to reach beyond his ACC dreams, when the Mets selected him in the first round of the 2001 draft. "I was fortunate that I had college coaches and professional scouts coming to see me play," he recalls. "I talked with the people who scheduled my classes to see if we could shuffle a few things here and there to get out a little early so that I could go out and take batting practice before my games in front of the scouts. I wanted to make sure that I did everything I could to put myself in a position to showcase the skills I had. It worked out really well for me."

The fact that his team has fallen short of its goals the past two seasons undoubtedly eats away at Wright, but he has learned to put his displeasure to good use. "My biggest motivation comes when I think about failing the past couple seasons as a team," he says, "When you fail, don't get the job done or underachieve, that's what gets me going and that's what fuels me. I want to go out there and be considered an unselfish player. If the team needs something, I'll give up an at-bat or I'll put myself in a position where I try to give myself up for the good of the team."

As a young star, team leader, and role model on a big-market team, Wright has been exposed to huge amounts of pressure at an early age. But even carrying the world's largest city on his back doesn't seem to shake him. "Obviously in New York, winning is first," he says. "Nothing else matters if you don't win. The fans don't care what you do individually if the team doesn't win and succeed. But I put a lot more pressure on myself than any sort of outside influence could ever put on me."

Training

Although Wright spends countless hours lifting weights and conditioning his body for each season, he is quick to point out his top priority. "You talk a lot about what you do in the weight room to build up your baseball muscles," he says. "But the best way to get in baseball shape is to go play the game. Long toss, taking swings, fielding ground balls, that's how you work all the little muscles that are tough to work in the weight room."

Wright always has a goal in mind when he sets out for his on-field training. "Baseball is so much about muscle memory that everything you practice has to carry over into the game," he says. "You really have to go out there with a purpose to work on stuff, because if you create bad habits, that will carry over into the game. You have to go game speed all the time. That has helped me focus a lot on quickness. I want to fire a little faster and be more explosive. I want to make sure that my first step is quick, and with hitting, my first movement is powerful and I get a good torque."

On-Field Warm-Up

Before he even thinks about performing baseball skills at game speed, Wright gets his body ready with a thorough on-field warm-up. "I do a lot of stretching, because it's tough to go out there and compete and play at your best if you have a nagging injury," he says. "It's important to loosen up your muscles before you go into the baseball skills. This warm-up is focused on getting a good sweat and lather

working; it's kind of two things in one. You get a good stretch but you also stay active and get the blood going with movement and plyometric work."

Base Running

Although his main strengths lie elsewhere, Wright has swiped a more-than-respectable 49 bases over the past two seasons due to his diligent base-path work. Another testament to his thorough game preparation and baseball intelligence is the fact that Wright routinely devotes several minutes each skill session to reading and reacting to a pitcher's delivery. This helps him avoid getting caught off guard and ensures he can take advantage of even the slightest miscue by an opposing hurler.

Arm Strength

One of the more difficult actions of playing the hot corner is making the cross-field throw to first base—especially after running or diving toward the third base line to field a sharply hit ball. Wright and his cannon are prepared. "It's somewhat of a long throw to begin with," he says. "So I really have to work on lengthening things out and making sure that come game time, my shoulder's strong enough to get it across the diamond. We do a lot of shoulder exercises to strengthen our arms and work on our throwing, but mainly the long toss is what strengthens it."

Early on in spring training, when soreness is more likely, Wright recommends performing Long Toss two or three times per week, with a focus on getting air underneath the ball until your arm gets into shape.

Fielding

Wright's Gold Gloves in 2007 and 2008 are proof that he's a complete baseball player.

"Taking ground balls is very important, because to me, defense and pitching win a lot of games," he says. "Everybody wants to hit, because that's where you get all the glory—for hitting home runs and driving in runs—but defense is where you can really help a pitcher out."

To make sure that he is ready for anything hit his way, Wright loads up the first part of spring training with a high volume of fielding drills. "At the very beginning of spring training, you take your most ground balls," he says. "You want to get your legs in shape and get your mind right so that you know what you have to work on moving forward to the end of spring training. By the end, you should have a pretty good idea of what you need to get ready before a game and what you need to work on in practice."

Wright's main focus on fielding comes down to soft hands and precise footwork. "I do a lot of one-handed drills where I try to make my hands as soft as possible so that my hand gives with the ball," he says. "Then, I back up and do some ground balls and really work on my footwork. I make sure that once I catch the ball, I can get my momentum going toward first base to make nice, strong throws. When you think about fielding a ground ball, you think about using your glove and hands. But you get into position with your feet, and that's why we do a lot of agility and plyometric work, to get our feet moving a little quicker and to get into position a little quicker. It doesn't matter how soft your hands are. If you don't get yourself into position, a lot of times you're going to miss the ground ball."

Hitting

The fact that Wright has hit over .300 in all four of his full seasons in the majors is a product of his always mindful work at the plate. "My batting practice starts before I take the field," he says. "I go down to the cage and hit off the tee for a little bit and then take a little Front Toss to get loosened up and get my hands activated. I carry that onto the field."

Once he steps up to the plate to put everything together, Wright sets out to achieve something with every cut. "My strength is going up the middle or [going] the other way, so the first rounds, I really work on keeping my hands inside the ball, trying to hit line drives to right-center. The last couple rounds, I try to hit the ball wherever it's pitched and really try to let loose. I pretend like I'm in game situations where I'm thinking to myself, 'Bottom of the ninth, and I really need to drive this run in.' I really try to focus each every pitch on accomplishing something."

Regarding technique, Wright knows his own swing inside and out. "For me, it's all about timing and being quick. I want to make sure I get my stride foot down early. I want to make sure that I have a nice rhythm going. . . . I don't want to feel like it's taking a while for the bat barrel to get to the strike zone."

Soft hands are great for fielding, but when it comes to wielding lumber, Wright seeks to harden up his old meat hooks. "You want to get your hands in shape and get those callouses, so I take the most swings early on. I want to get comfortable handling the bat so that I can pull [the ball] when I want to pull it and hit it the other way if I want to. As we get further into spring training, we cut down on the volume and start working on specific things. Toward the end, I take about 50 swings total. If I can go in there and take 50 good, solid swings where I feel comfortable going into the game, I'd rather do that than continuously hack and get into some bad habits."

ON-FIELD WARM-UP

Perform the following movements and stretches in consecutive fashion upon taking the field. The warm-up should take approximately 15 minutes to complete.

SINGLE-LEG DUMBBELL SQUAT

- Jog/Backpedal

- Run, Pivot, Run

- Front-to-Back Leg Swings

- Side-to-Side Leg Swings

- Saigon Squat

- Trunk Rotations

- Arm Circles

- Straddle Stretch [right, left, middle]

- Groin Stretch

- Hip Flexor Stretch [in Lunge position]

- Shoulder Stretch [arm across chest]

- Lat/Triceps Stretch [elbow to sky]

- Overhead Reach and Twist [arms overhead and twist]

- Walking Lunge

- Straight-Leg March

- Shuffle/Groin Stretch
  [two shuffles, Lateral Lunge each direction; repeat]

- Butt Kicks

- Power Skips

BASERUNNING

"IN THE DIRT" READ AND REACT

- Assume lead at first base

- Perform two shuffles as teammate or coach simulates pitcher's delivery

- Read location of pitch to determine course of action

- If ball is in dirt, turn and sprint to second base

- If ball is caught by catcher, quickly return to first base

- Repeat for specified reps

- Perform at second base

COACHING POINTS

➡ Stay low during shuffles
➡ Work with both left- and right-handed pitchers

ARM STRENGTH

Early on in spring training, when soreness is more likely, David recommends performing the long toss two or three times per week with a focus on getting air underneath the ball until your arm gets into shape.

LONG TOSS

- Begin playing catch with partner about 10 yards away

- After each throw, take a small step back

- Continue to distance that challenges longest possible throw

- Finish by performing a few hard throws from about 20 yards away

Reps: 1–2 throws at each distance

FIELDING

1 ONE-HANDED FIELDING

- Assume fielding position with coach or teammate about 40 feet away

- As partner hits grounders, approach ball and field it with glove hand only

COACHING POINTS

- ➡ Get into fielding position quickly with feet
- ➡ Stay low
- ➡ Focus on keeping fielding hand soft and allow it to give with ball

2 GROUND BALLS

- Assume fielding position with coach or teammate at home plate

- As partner hits hard grounders, approach ball and field it

- Quickly throw ball to first base

COACHING POINTS

- ➡ Get into fielding position quickly with feet
- ➡ Stay low
- ➡ Focus on soft hands and allow them to give with ball
- ➡ Get momentum going toward first to add strength to throw

HITTING

1 TEE BALL

- Assume batting stance at plate with tee in front

- Take controlled swings with proper path to ball

2 FRONT TOSS

- Assume batting stance at plate

- As partner tosses balls underhand from behind L-screen 20 feet away, take controlled swings with proper path to ball

3 LIVE BATTING PRACTICE

- Assume batting stance at plate

- As partner throws ball overhand from behind L-screen 40 feet away, take controlled swings with proper path to ball

COACHING POINTS

- ➡ Have specific focus for each pitch
- ➡ Get stride foot down early
- ➡ Try to get into rhythm
- ➡ Focus on quick, short swing

DAVID WRIGHT'S TRAINING GUIDE

ON-FIELD WARM-UP	SETS	REPS/DISTANCE
Perform the following movements and stretches in consecutive fashion upon taking the field. The warm-up should take about 15 minutes to complete.		
Jog/Backpedal	2	20 yards each
Run, Pivot, Run	2	20 yards
Front-to-Back Leg Swings	1	10 each leg
Side-to-Side Leg Swings	1	10 each leg
Saigon Squat	1	20 seconds
Trunk Rotations	1	10 each direction
Arm Circles	1	10 each direction
Straddle Strech	1	20 seconds each direction
Groin Stretch	1	20 seconds each leg
Hip Flexor Stretch	1	20 seconds each leg
Shoulder Stretch	1	20 seconds each arm
Lat/Tricep Stretch	1	20 seconds each arm
Overhead Reach and Twist	1	10 each direction
Walking Lunge	1	20 yards
Straight-Leg March	1	20 yards
Shuffle/Groin Stretch	1	20 yards
Butt Kicks	1	20 yards
Power Skips	1	20 yards

BASERUNNING	REPS/DISTANCE
"In The Dirt" Read and React	5–10 at each base

ARM STRENGTH	REPS/DISTANCE
Long Toss	1–2 throws at each distance

FIELDING	REPS/DISTANCE
One-Handed Fielding	10 to 15
Ground Balls	10 to 20

HITTING	SETS	REPS/DISTANCE
Tee Ball	2–3	10–15
Front Toss	2–3	10–15
Live Batting Practice	2–3	10

RECOMMENDED RESOURCES

STACK

For the Athlete, By the Athlete

Originally founded as a magazine, STACK has developed into a fully diversified multimedia company providing information and advice on athletic training, nutrition, and sports skills from top professional and collegiate athletes and coaches on the following major brand platforms:

STACK Media is one of the top sports properties on the Internet, with an average of 4 million unique visitors and 100 million page views per month. Combining its editorial content with product and service offerings from several partner sites in a distributed media network, STACK Media has become the acknowledged leader in reaching its audience of active sports participants online.

STACK.com, the digital home for all STACK content and Web-based tools, is one of the Internet's fastest-growing sites, delivering information exclusively for the active sports community.

STACK TV, an online video platform with eight channels of unique, originally produced videos, provides the largest library of sports performance video content on the Web.

STACK **Magazine**, requested by more than 9,000 high school athletic directors, has a circulation of 800,000 and a readership of more than 5 million high school athletes.

MySTACK, a social network and recruiting site, allows athletes to create profiles with their personal information and stats, upload highlight films and photos, and send their profiles to college coaches to take control of the recruiting process.

Eastbay

Eastbay.com

The leading supplier of athletic footwear, apparel, and training gear, Eastbay.com and its direct mail catalog are essential resources for athletes interested in the top brands, including Nike, Reebok, adidas, and others. As marketing partners, STACK and Eastbay share the goal of helping high school and college athletes meet all of their performance needs. Through Eastbay Training Centers, presented by STACK on Eastbay.com, the retailer offers the latest and greatest in sport performance content as well as its traditional product lines.

beRecruited.com

Founded in 2000 by a former collegiate athlete, beRecruited.com provides a platform for high school student-athletes to connect and interact with college coaches across the nation. More than 200,000 registered student-athletes use beRecruited.com to build online profiles and evaluate opportunities to take their game to the next level. STACK creates content to inform high school athletes of the recruiting process, while beRecruited offers an environment in which athletes can apply their skills and knowledge to achieve their recruiting goals.

Varsity Networks, Inc.

varsitynetworks.com

Varsity Networks helps more than 9,000 high schools across the country manage, motivate, and stay connected with their teams. Users are able to post commentary, video, photos, and team stats to the site. The company also distributes content to local and national media outlets to feature on-air or on their websites. Varsity Network's services have value for all members of the high school sports community, including athletic directors, coaches, players, parents, and fans.

iHigh.com

iHigh.com, Inc. offers free services to high schools and student-athletes throughout the United States, allowing them to create and maintain their own branded websites. Through iHigh.com, teams and news organizations are able to post live broadcasts, stories, photos, and videos to their customized team pages. Student-athletes can also set up individual profiles through the social network myihigh.com. The iHigh site features the first national network of member schools in one comprehensive online destination.

RECRUITING RESOURCES

National Collegiate Athletic Association

ncaa.org

The NCAA's official website houses its Eligibility Center, which provides information and resources for prospective collegiate student-athletes. The NCAA Eligibility Center offers a guide for college-bound student-athletes, lists of approved high school academic requirements, and provides registration forms. Also available at ncaa.org is information on legislation and governance, statistics, and records for all NCAA sports and a comprehensive library of NCAA publications and journals.

NUTRITION RESOURCES

Gatorade Sports Science Institute [GSSI]

gssiweb.com

GSSI is a research facility dedicated to sharing the latest information about exercise science and sports nutrition. In an effort to expand education about enhancing athletic performance, the Institute provides services and tools for athletes and sports health professionals, and develops state-of-the-art technology used by the nation's principal scientists who are committed to furthering sports nutrition research.